A Genre in Hindusthani Music (Bhajans) as Used in the Roman Catholic Church

A Genre in Hindusthani Music (Bhajans) as Used in the Roman Catholic Church

Stephen F. Duncan

Roman Catholic Studies
Volume 12

The Edwin Mellen Press
Lewiston•Queenston•Lampeter

Library of Congress Cataloging-in-Publication Data

Duncan, Stephen F.
  A genre in Hindusthani music (bhajans) as used in the Roman
Catholic Church / Stephen F. Duncan : foreword by John David
Peterson.
      p. cm.-- (Roman Catholic studies ; v. 12)
  Includes bibliographical references (p.   ), discography (p.   ),
and index.
  ISBN 0-7734-8273-3
  1. Church music--India--20th century. 2. Church music--Catholic
Church--20th century. 3. Bhajans, Hindi--History and criticism.
I. Series.
ML3051.I4D86   1999
782.32'. 22' 00954--dc21

                                                          98-47116
                                                            CIP
                                                            MN

This is volume 12 in the continuing series
Roman Catholic Studies
Volume 12 ISBN 0-7734-8273-3
RCS Series ISBN 0-88946-240-X

A CIP catalog record for this book is available from the British Library.

The Edwin Mellen Press   The Edwin Mellen Press
      Box 450   Box 67
Lewiston, New York   Queenston, Ontario
  USA 14092-0450   CANADA L0S 1L0

The Edwin Mellen Press, Ltd.
Lampeter, Ceredigion, Wales
UNITED KINGDOM SA48 8LT

Printed in the United States of America

For my parents,
Mr. & Mrs. Rusty and Marian Duncan,
without whose love and encouragement
my journey would have never taken me to India

TABLE OF CONTENTS

LIST OF FIGURES

LIST OF EXAMPLES

iv

ACKNOWLEDGEMENTS

The author is indebted to the following individuals and institutions for their assistance in the completion of this project:

Ms. Anna Szatowski, Ms. Alice Olson, Ms. Maurine Brooks, Ms. Ersie Harden and Rev. David Knight for their help in the prosaic matters involved in traveling to India and keeping house while completing the project.

Sr. Dolores McKinney, C.N.D. for her help in travel coordination, bookkeeping, and research assistance.

Rev. Maurice D'Souza, C.S.C. for the suggestion and invitation to travel to India and to the Priests, Brothers and Sisters of Holy Cross serving in India for their marvelous hospitality in Bangalore, Pune, Bombay, Tiruchchirappalli, Madurai and Tanjore.

Rev. Dr. Charles Vas, S.V.D., D. Mus., and all those involved at *Sangeet Abhinay Academy* in Bandra for their invaluable assistance in learning *bhajan* and *kirtan* forms as well as *Hindusthani* theory.

Rev. Augustine Silvera, S.J., and the staff of the *Jesuit Retreat House* in Bandra for providing the author with such a wonderful place to stay while studying at *Sangeet Abhinay Academy.*

Rev. Jacob Thekanath, Rev. Paul Puthanangady, S.D.B., Sr. Jacinta and the staff of the *National Biblical, Catechetical and Liturgical Centre* in Bangalore for their hospitality, information and publications.

Rev. Dr. John Edapilly and the staff of *Dharmarum* Seminary in Bangalore for their help with the Syrian connection.

Rev. Dr. Subash Annand of the *Jnana Deepa Vidyapeeth Papal Seminary* in Pune for his assistance with Hindu philosophy.

Rev. Arulraj Gali, C.S.C. for Tamil translations and transliterations.

Mr. Paul Gray for his help with the philosophical and theological matters concerning the Second Vatican Council.

Most Rev. Ibrahim N. Ibrahim, bishop of the *Eparchy of St. Thomas the Apostle,* Catholic Chaldean Diocese in the United States for his information regarding the current status of the Chaldeans.

Aswan Tejwani and Dr. Prashant Palvia (Memphis State University) for their help in editing the Hindi texts and corrections in the Devengari script.

Kalai Kauvery in Tiruchiappali, *Ishvani Kendra* in Pune, The Daughters of St. Paul in India, *Dharmarum Seminary* and *Sangeet Abhinay Academy* for recording and publishing Christian *Bhajans.*

Excerpts from the publications of *Sangeet Abhinay Academy* used with permission. All rights reserved.

FOREWORD

Many times Christian music has taken as its ideal the music of a time and place not its own. Sometimes this has to do with heritage, as when a church musician of the Episcopal Church (U.S.A.) takes British music as a model. Sometimes, though, it seems that the culture of Western art and music has been included in the package with the conversion of non-Western peoples to Christianity. So we find, for instance, Asian hymns that can only be distinguished from American Gospel hymns by the language of their texts.

Dr. Duncan's book is an exploration of an indigenous musical tradition applied to the Roman Catholic liturgy since the Second Vatican Council. Its traversal of Hindu music and the convoluted history of organized Christianity in India puts into perspective the need for and the practice of a Christian liturgy adorned the rich musical heritage of Indian tradition.

There is strength here, and simplicity. There is a refined and deep appreciation of the theoretical complexities and the rarefied beauty of Indian music. And there is a sense of holy adventure, a delight in telling the old story in a way that is new to Westerners. Ironically, this "new way" is found through music that is older than much traditional Western music and may even be older than the story itself.

And so we limited beings are again reminded of the limitless love and unfathomable power of the Divine transcending place and time.

I will bring your offspring from the east,

and from the west I will gather you;

I will say to the north,

 Give up,

and to the south,

Do not withhold;

bring my sons from afar

and my daughters from the end of the earth,

every one who is called by my name,

whom I created for my glory,

whom I formed and made.

(Isa. 43: 5-7, Revised Standard Version)

John David Peterson, DMA August 1998

You may be surprised to learn that Christianity came to India long before it went to England or Western Europe, and when even in Rome it was a despised and proscribed sect. Within 100 years of the death of Jesus, Christian missionaries came to South India by sea. They were received courteously and permitted to preach their new faith. They converted a large number of people, and their descendants have lived there, with varying fortunes, to this day.

Jawaharlal Nehru

CHAPTER 1

INTRODUCTION

Music has long been one of the most important and powerful aids to the worship life of the Catholic Church. It serves to accompany ritual action, to gather the local community, to provide a sense of belonging, to encourage reverence and to give voice to religious feeling that is beyond speech. The Second Vatican Council in dealing with liturgy and music sought to make both of them more accessible to the faithful. The fathers of the Council permitted the use of the vernacular languages as well as the local genius of the peoples. The Church responded by seeking to incarnate itself in the local community. Ritual actions were modified by competent authority, music was composed in familiar styles and the arts of the local inhabitants began to be used more fully by the Church.

In the West, the changes were not drastic. The altar was turned, the language was changed, but the culture remained that of Western Europe. In the mission lands (whose cultures were often more ancient than those of Europe) the changes were remarkable. Non-Western peoples were both allowed and encouraged to use the culture and traditions of their lands in their worship. Native dress, musical instruments and architecture were borrowed or adapted and a renewal of the worship life of the Church began.

This study is historical in nature. It approaches the present situation on the subcontinent of India through the documents of the Second Vatican Council along with the Post-Conciliar documents of the Roman Curia and the documents of the Catholic Bishops' Conference of India (C.B.C.I.). The C.B.C.I.'s choice to approach the cultural world of the Hindu's requires a basic understanding of the forces acting within Hindu philosophy and theology, especially as these impact upon ritual and ritual music. The development of the *Bhakti* (devotion) Path within Hinduism gave rise to two musical forms that have been adopted by the Catholic Church in India: *bhajan* and *kirtan*. Understanding of these forms requires a basic understanding of Indian music theory (both in *Ragas,* melodic formulas, and *Talas,* rhythm patterns). With this understanding it is possible to examine the current uses of these prayer forms and to offer some commentary on the future of these inculturized forms within the Church.

The history of indigenous music in the worship life of the Catholic Church in India is long and complex. There are numerous factors involved which include: the cultures of the various peoples of India, the influences of the Reformation and the Counter-Reformation, the schisms from the early history of the Church, the divisions between East and West, and many other socio-political factors. *Bhajan* and *kirtan* existed in the Hindu temple long before the Catholic Church allowed their use in its liturgy.

Tradition maintains that St. Thomas, the apostle, traveled to India, founded the Church there, and was martyred near Madras. The early Christian community had ties with the Church in Bhagdad (the Patriarchate of Selucia-Ctesiphon), which also was founded by St. Thomas. By the third century it is known that the liturgy was celebrated not in the native Indian languages, but in Syrian. The Portuguese Jesuits arrived at the height of the Counter-Reformation and brought with them a Catholicism of strict Latin imitation. A division between two factions of the Syrian Christians of India occurred under the administration of the Portuguese. The majority followed the edicts of the Latins and are known as the Syro-Malabar Christians. With the Synod of Diamper in June 1599, the Syro-Malabar Christians were removed from the jurisdiction of the patriarch of Selucia-Ctesiphon and were placed directly under papal jurisdiction. A minority refused to serve under the Jesuits and established the Syro-Malankara Rite with the permission of the Jacobite Patriarch of Antioch. For almost five hundred years the Catholic Church in India (and throughout the world) maintained a fortress mentality regarding change. There was one Church, one faith, one language, and one liturgy.[1]

During the twentieth century some of the Syro-Malankara bishops petitioned Rome for full communion with the Holy See. The Syro-Malankarans who were returned to papal jurisdiction were allowed to keep their Antiochean liturgy (which was in Malayalam, the vernacular language of Kerela). Also during the twentieth century, the Syro-Malabar liturgy was restored to its Seleucian form. The Syro-

---

[1]For a more detailed history of these Rites see Appendix C: A Brief History of Catholicism in India.

Malabar petitioned Rome for permission to use Malayalam as a liturgical language. Rome approved, allowing both the Syro-Malabar and the Syro-Malankara liturgies to be celebrated in the vernacular. By the beginning of the Second Vatican Council there were three Rites in India: The Latin Rite, the Syro-Malabar Rite and the Syro-Malankara Rite. At the Second Vatican Council bishops from the two indigenous Rites spoke eloquently on the use of vernacular languages in liturgy.[2]

---

[2]Strictly speaking there were several Rites, but the Church in the West (Rome) believed that all should be done as it was in the Latin Rite.

CHAPTER 2
THE SECOND VATICAN COUNCIL

The Second Vatican Council was convoked by Pope John XXIII to "open up the windows and let the fresh air in." No single event since the implementation of the Council of Trent had had such an impact upon the life and worship of the Church. The Fathers of the Council examined the life of the Church in many ways. They commented upon the past, expressed hopes for the future and made changes in the present day. The first document, *Sacrosanctum Concilium*, was promulgated on December 4, 1963. This *Constitution on the Sacred Liturgy* was to fundamentally re-evaluate the public worship of the Church. Stated in the first few pages of this document is the principle change: According to Article 14 the participation of the assembly fully and actively is to be considered before anything else. Their participation is essential since it is through their participation that the liturgy interacts with their lives. The liturgy is the source and summit of their spiritual progress as Christians.

Full and active participation is not easily accomplished when the assembly is speaking to God in a language other than their mother-tongue.[3] Neither is it simple when the metaphors and symbols used in their religious services are not a part of their cultural tradition.[4] Because of this the Council allowed changes and adaptations into the liturgy that are consistent with the teachings of the Church and bring people to a greater understanding of the mysteries. In Article 21 the Council provides the outline of restoration of the liturgy. The essential and unchanging elements are to be restored with the restorations executed so as to make the texts and the rites more accessible to the assembly. The participation as a worshipping community is encouraged with the statement that the assembly should be able to do so with ease. In Article 30 various musical activities and physical activities are singled out as belonging to the assembly. It should surprise no one that these included songs, acclamations, hymns, psalms, responses and antiphons.

---

[3]It is often said that people pray, curse and count money in their mother tongue.

[4]The concept "white as snow" only makes complete sense to someone who has seen snow.

Since music as an art has been held in great esteem by the church through the centuries, the Council addressed Sacred Music as a chapter in and of itself. Article 112 begins by pointing out that music has always been highly treasured by the Church. An art which is considered pre-eminent among the others precisely because it combines sacred text with music as an integrated part of the liturgy. Sacred music is then in effect more holy when it reflects the meanings of the texts and actions to which it is related. The Church clearly approves of all art which can be used for the liturgy. [5] Furthermore, Article 113 specifically states that the liturgy is ennobled through the use of music with the ministers and the assembly working together in song. Specific use of languages is set out in Articles 36 for the Mass, 54 for the sacraments, and 63 for the Liturgy of the Hours.

Article 36 allowed the use of the vernacular in the Mass and the sacraments because it often was of great advantage to the assembly. Article 54 encourages the use of the vernacular in the readings and the common prayer of the assembly. Article 63 set into motion a series of translations of the sacraments and sacramentals into the various vernacular languages. Article 101 maintained the Latin language for the Liturgy of the Hours in the Latin rite. This could be dispensed with by the local ordinary or competent superior. The vernacular translation used still had to be approved by the Roman Curia.

Another section of the Constitution acknowledges the genius of the local people including particularly their culture and traditions. Article 119 begins by stating that particularly in the mission lands the local traditions and culture are to be respected. Music of the local people is to be adapted for use within the liturgy of the Church. It continues by exhorting that the preparation of all missionaries include their training in the indigenous musical traditions. [6]

Following these basic guidelines set by the Council, a post-Conciliar instruction was issued on March 5, 1967 that contained much more detailed

---

[5]Flannery, p. 32.

[6]Flannery, p. 33.

instructions and directions for growth. Some of these instructions are of great importance for the introduction of indigenous music into the Church in India. Section 9 states that no style of music is prohibited for use in sacred liturgy so long as it is capable of supporting the spirit of the liturgical action and does not form an impediment to the participation of the assembly. [7]

In considering the ministry of music and musical leadership the instruction states in Section 21 that there should be trained singers, especially when there is no choir, to assist the assembly. This leader can both lead and support the faithful. Such a leader [cantor] is useful even when there is a choir. The assembly is expected to participate in the musical settings of the Ordinary and the musical settings of the Proper as set forth in the liturgy. [8] The choir is encouraged to sing, but never when such singing would serve to exclude the assembly from their rightful place in the Ordinary. [9]

Regarding Sacraments and Sacramentals the instruction admonishes ministers in Section 46 that for popular devotions music may be drawn form the old and the newer heritage of sacred music. Musical instruments are allowed in a supporting role including such as are "characteristic of a particular people." [10] Section 61 points out that experts in music will be needed in the preparation of music for the liturgy in mission lands. Such experts will need background both in liturgy and in the music of the people. [11] Section 63 forbids the use of any instrument which is held to be "suitable for secular music only." [12]

---

[7]Flannery, pp. 82-3.

[8]Flannery, p. 86.

[9]Flannery, p. 88.

[10]Flannery, p. 91.

[11]Flannery, p. 95.

[12]Flannery, p. 96.

Section 69 calls for the creation of liturgical commissions to oversee the work of restoration of the liturgy in various places. Such commissions are encouraged to work not just in their own country but with others who may have the same interests and needs. In India, this liturgical committee was established by the Catholic Bishops' Committee of India and has overseen the implementation of the directives of the Fathers of the Council. [13]

---

[13]Flannery, p. 97.

CHAPTER 3
THE CATHOLIC BISHOPS' CONFERENCE OF INDIA
AFTER VATICAN II

In India, the C.B.C.I. established its Liturgical commission based upon the documents of the Council and Canon law regarding authority. Of this foundation Rev. Dr. Amalorpavadass wrote that the Constitution on the Sacred Liturgy gave authority to the local bishops' conferences and that the C.B.C.I. understood its responsibilities regarding liturgical reform. [14] In April of 1964, the majority of bishops approved the use of the vernacular in all parts of the Mass except the *Canon*.[15] In October of 1966, the General Meeting of the C.B.C.I. was held in New Delhi. During this meeting the bishops decided that liturgy and catechetics were to be central to the pastoral care of the faithful. The bishops established a Liturgical Commission and the National Centre for Catechetics and Liturgy in Bangalore (National Biblical, Catechetical and Liturgical Centre: N.B.C.L.C.).[16] At the same meeting the bishops agreed that the adaptation of the liturgy should include:

(i) respect for the Christian message and worship;

(ii) research into the common rituals of non-Christians in India
    (Muslim as well as Hindu);

(iii) adaptation and experimentation can only be attempted with permission   of the local ordinary and the regional conference of bishops [17]

---

[14]Father D. S. Amalorpavadass, ed., *Post Vatican II Liturgical Renewal in India (1963-1968)* (Bangalore, India: N.B.C.L.C., 1968), p. iii.

[15]*Post Vatican II Liturgical Renewal in India (1963-1968)*, p. 1.

[16]*Post Vatican II Liturgical Renewal in India (1963-1968)*, p. vii.

[17]*Post Vatican II Liturgical Renewal in India (1963-1968)*, p. 8.

By July of 1967 the C.B.C.I. recommended the entire Mass be permitted in the vernacular. It also recommended work in adaptation of music for these vernacular texts. Three of the important points are paraphrased here:

(a) That new vernacular melodies be composed.
(b) That melodies for the minister's portions must be approved by the   Regional Conferences of Bishops (C.B.C.I. for English).
(c) That musicians be encouraged to submit vernacular melodies which can   then sorted through by the regional bishops' conference for suitability for use throughout the country. [18]

The C.B.C.I. also proposed and passed a resolution for the creation of a School for Hindusthani Music as well as another for Carnatic music with the Chair of the Liturgical Commission being empowered to raise funds to support the project.[19]

In February of 1968 the C.B.C.I. Sub-Commission for Music made several statements on the composition of sacred music in the vernacular languages of India. They were concerned that a single center be established where the approved vernacular texts could be filed and from where composers could order copies. It was also recommended that compositions completed in the vernacular should be collected and available also from a single center or at least published in the journal *Word and Worship*. The Commission noted that there were two schools for the teaching of Hindusthani music already in existence. Encouraged by the C.B.C.I. is the Northern School of Hindusthani Music founded by Fr. Edmond. It was affiliated with the *Prayag Sangit Samiti* and was directed then by Fr. Vijayanand. The Bombay School of Hindusthani Music founded by Fr. G. Proksch, S.V.D. was affiliated with a College of Music in Lucknow. Students in Bombay could study voice, tabla, sitar, harmonium, flute and

---

[18]*Post Vatican II Liturgical Renewal in India (1963-1968)*, pp. 86-7.

[19]*Post Vatican II Liturgical Renewal in India (1963-1968)*, pp. 86-7.

dance. Six music teachers were involved with this school at the time. While there were no schools for Carnatic musicians, the Conference supported the idea of creating one. Further the Conference was concerned that the schools not merely teach Indian music, but help Catholic composers to create indiginized music for the use of Catholic Christians in India. They commented that there was much room for traveling teachers who could spread this music across the country. Local schools and summer sessions were also mentioned. [20]

The C.B.C.I. after establishing these suggestions went on with the business of implementing the changes required by the Second Vatican Council and the overseeing of translations into many languages of these changes. That there is little published regarding music is not surprising. The Church has encouraged music as art and as prayer for centuries. The permission to use indigenous music was accepted by some, rejected by others and ignored by many. The bishops did not enforce a particular style of music on any community.[21] Rather they allowed the use of indigenized music and musical instruments where the local community would find it helpful.

In 1980 the N.B.C.L.C. sponsored a Seminar for Composers of Liturgical Music. This seminar gathered together musicians from across the subcontinent. Several conclusions were included in the published statement of the seminar and are worth paraphrasing here.

> People who understand that the entirety of creation is good having come into existence through the Word of God[22], and knowing that all of creation has been redeemed by this same

---

[20]*Post Vatican II Liturgical Renewal in India (1963-1968)*, pp. 115-6.

[21]The author experienced Indian communities singing a variety of music: American Gospel, English Victorian song, Roman (Gregorian) Chant, Syrian Chant, *Glory and Praise* and even the works of Brother John Michael Talbot in addition to Hindusthani and Karnatic music.

[22]Christ Jesus, "Word of the Father."

Word made flesh, acknowledge that there are problems in deciding what is sacred and what is profane in music. Certainly not all music is suited for liturgical celebration, but that is a question of function, not of style. [23] At this beginning what is needed is the realization that all styles of music and all musical instruments are in themselves good. They have the potential to express faith and to be used in liturgy. Since the mission of Christ is universal, the indigenization of music is not some kind of hobby, rather it is a timely responsibility. One made more important by the great influence music holds in our religious and social lives. For these reasons we note the variety of styles found in Western music as well as those found in Hindusthani, Carnatic and tribal musics. Those musical traditions which are already religious lend themselves to adaptation more easily, but all styles can be used for the expression of faith in worship. We must decide which hymn, *bhajan, namjap, kirtan, namvali, sloka,* etc. Is the best choice for use in a particular place in the liturgy and in a particular season of the liturgical year. In the end all new music created must be written to show both fidelity to faith and the beauty of indigenized prayer.[24]

The musician participants were convinced that a truly indigenous Indian Liturgical Music should reflect the musical styles of India as well as the liturgy. In particular the raga used should reflect the meaning of the text which it supports. This would include the season of the year and the time of day as will be explained further in the section on *ragas* and *rasas.*

---

[23]Not all music is suitable for the functions of the liturgy. For more on this see Stephen F. Duncan, *Ritual Music for the Roman Catholic Church: A Problem of Practicality and Æsthetics,* (Memphis, Tennessee: Diocese of Memphis in Tennessee, 1989).

[24]Catholic Bishops Conference of India, *Conclusions of the Seminar for Composers of Liturgical Music* (Bangalore, India: N.B.C.L.C., 1980), p. 2-3.

Hinduism and the Catholic Church

The bishops in India have begun to study and adapt religious traditions from the native peoples of India. Though this is primarily an issue of liturgy, it is also in the spirit of the Second Vatican Council's "Declaration on the Relation of the Church to Non-Christian Religions" (*Nostra Ætate*) in which the Council acknowledged the truth found in many of the great religions of the world and noted in particular the philosophies found in Hinduism.[25]

Non-Christian cultures, then, can provide authentic expressions of worship. Where these are congruent with Catholic teaching they may be adopted, where they are not exactly the same as the Christian teachings they may be adapted to a Christo-centric view. The C.B.C.I. has begun programs of study and adaptation of the various cultures of India. Since Hinduism comprises the bulk of Indian history, it has been approached first. Work within the animist (tribal) areas continues as does work with the other major religions (Buddhist, Sikh, Moslem, and Jain). The C.B.C.I. through the All-India Liturgical Meetings (A.I.L.M.) has outlined a course involving two basic phases for inculturation of the liturgies of the Church. In the first phase, relatively simple changes were proposed that would allow a more Indian atmosphere in the celebrations. In the second phase more radical adaptations were proposed which include a deeper inculturation.

The first set of adaptations was approved by Rome in 1969. Commonly referred to as the 12 Points of Adaptation (See Appendix A-- Official Document of the Holy See), these inculturations allow the celebrating community to use a number of uniquely Indian gestures as well as vestments. They include: 1) Removal of footwear and use of Indian postures for the Mass; 2) The *anjali hasta*[26] with a profound bow instead of a genuflection; 3) A *panchanga pranam*[27] by the

---

[25]Flannery, pp. 738-9.

[26]In this gesture the hands are placed with the palms together and the base of the thumbs touching the forehead. It is a sign both of welcome and of respect. It is also used as a sign of peace.

[27]This gesture is made by kneeling on the floor and touching the forehead and hands also to the floor. The hands may also be placed together on the forehead (as in the *anjali hasta*) and touched to

faithful during the penitential rite and at the end of the *anaphora*; 4) Touching an object of veneration and then bringing the fingertips to one's forehead replaces the kissing of objects of veneration; 5) The kiss of peace is replaced by the *anjali hasta* or the Syrian custom of placing the hands of the giver between the hands of the receiver; 6) The Indian incense bowl with handle may replace the *thurible*; 7) A simple tunic with stole or shawl may replace the elaborate (and hot) Roman and Syrian vestments; 8) A tray may replace the *corporal*; 9) Candles may be replaced with Indian oil lamps;[28] 10) The Preparatory Rites of the Mass may include a lighting of the lamp (*lucernarium*),[29] welcoming *arati* (waving of light, flowers or incense), presentation of the gifts, and sign of peace; 11) More freedom is allowed the assembly during the Prayer of the Faithful; 12) The use of the triple *arati* of flowers, incense and fire is allowed both at the Preparation of the Gifts and Altar and at the Great Doxology concluding the *Anaphora*.

Regarding these adaptations a number of the bishops of India raised important questions regarding the use of non-Western and non-Syrian cultural adaptations in the liturgies of the Church. These concerns stem from two basic sources. One is a desire to maintain the Liturgy as it has been understood for the past four hundred years. The other is a desire not to be identified with the Hindu cult by any identification with Hindu culture. Questions arose which are similar to those heard throughout the world during the revisions of the liturgy. Thoughts such as:

Indianization -- yes, but not Hinduization .

We are converting ourselves to Hinduism.

---

the floor. This is an Indian posture of penitence and awe.

[28]The sometimes angry discussions over this *change* seem strange since the early Church used oil lamps almost exclusively. The sanctuary lamps were usually run with the leftover holy oils from the last liturgical year.

[29]The lighting of the lamp (*lucernarium*) was a required part of celebration of Evening Prayer until the advent of electric lights. In both the East and the West it was often accompanied by the Greek hymn *Phos Hilaron* (Φῶς ἱλαρὸν) which gives thanks to Jesus as the Light of the world sent by the Father.

What need is there to take from Hinduism since Christianity is sufficient?

Why put away traditions which have served piety for centuries?[30] ...

Why should a small number of liturgists impose their will on a majority of believers? ...[31]

It should be noted that many of these concerns are the same as those of other bishops throughout the world. After almost four centuries of immutability the liturgy took on the character of timelessness. Only scholars and liturgists exhibited interest in the study of the earlier liturgy of the Church. Everyone else had been brought up to believe that this was *the* liturgy. While not dismissing these concerns, they may be considered a world-wide problem. The concerns over *Hinduization* seem equally strong. Some of the bishops and the laity seem to have believed that the liturgy was then to be adapted to Hinduism. It is important to remember that the liturgy is not adapted to fit the local culture. No one, not even a priest has permission to change the *anaphora* as set by the regional conference of bishops and approved by the Roman Curia.[32] Nor does anyone have permission to alter the words of the scriptures. Rather, the customs of the local culture are adapted for use in the liturgy of the Church. The local community using its arts and customs gives life to the liturgy of the Church.

---

[30]This comment is heard throughout the world regarding the changes after Vatican II. The Syrian Christian community in India had its own liturgy 1,000 years before the coming of the Latin Rite to India. They rightly assert that there was nothing wrong with their liturgy when the Portuguese came and changed it. The *Missale Romanum* promulgated by Pius V in his bull *Quo primum tempore* in 1570 included the reforms of the Council of Trent.

[31]Amolorpavadass, Towards Indigenisation in the Liturgy, pp. 8-10.

[32]In India, the Catholic Bishops' Conference of India (C.B.C.I.).

Music is one of the arts which the Church has borrowed from Hindu worship and adapted to its liturgies. Three basic divisions exist within Hinduism: knowledge (*Jnana*), religious works (*Karma*), and the path of devotion (*Bhakti*). The pursuits of Jnana tend to be scholarly and therefore are followed by a relatively few scholars or priests (*brahmins*) The works of *Karma* are often solitary with little or no prayer in common. The *Bhaktimarga*[33] life, with its path of devotion, a path based in faith, a path followed in love, is accessible to all.[34] The path of Bhakti is a path with celebrations (liturgies) held in common, a public gathering of the faithful. *Bhakti* would correspond roughly to the western notion of "devotion". The root of the word *Bhakti* is *bhaj,* meaning "partake." *Bhakti* theologically expresses no need for knowledge. As the *Bhakta*, or worshipper, sees the world, the main obstacle for the faithful is not a lack of knowledge, but a lack of belief. It is not possible for one to reason to God, for the human mind cannot grasp the infiniteness of *Brahman*. Therefore, one should abandon all thoughts of knowing God through mental processes or meditations. Likewise, *Bhakti* shows little need for works. The works of a human being can never merit the grace (*prasada*) of the loving God. While works may express one's love and devotion to God, they can not earn God's favor. The Hindu path of *karma* is negated then, for the forgiving grace of God is far beyond the sinfulness of humanity.

In *Bhakti* the devotee, *bhakta,* looks upon God as a person. As in human dynamics, there are many relationships possible. Modern *pooja*, worship, is a sacramentalization of human feeling. The icon chosen by the *Bhakta* (*Bhakti* follower) for God expresses the devotee's relationship with God. The devotee waits for a visit from God in the same way that one would await the arrival of a long expected guest. God is welcomed in love. One welcomes God as one would a friend. The devotee makes God a part of daily life at home as well as temple *pooja*. As with a guest in the home, God may be provided with new clothing. A bell is rung to awaken the guest, and so a bell may be used to "awaken" God to our presence. People sing and dance and entertain their God in the same way they

---

[33]"The way of devotion, faith, and love." Benjamin Walker, *The Hindu World: An Encyclopedic Survey of Hinduism* (New York: Frederick A. Praeger, Publishers, 1968), p. 139.

[34]Kshiti Mohan Sen, *Hinduism* (London: Penguin Books Limited: 1961), p. 20.

would entertain a friend. Rubrics are thus exchanged for hospitality, and hospitality itself becomes ritual.

Bhakti implies several things of the devotee: 1) a belief in a God which is personal and loving, 2) a personal love of God which consumes the devotee, 3) absolute devotion to and absolute faith in God, 4) self-surrender to the will of God, 5) approaching God for refuge and protection, 6) a real belief in the divinity of the human soul and the willingness of God to protect, love and save those who are devoted.

This accessible approach to God helps to explain the appeal and strength of *Bhakti*. The music of the *Bhakti* rituals is called *samvet bhajan*. This is a choral music which is simple enough for the active participation of all the *bhaktas* present. It calls for simple repetitious phrases with uncomplicated melodies. Though the musical prayer form of the *bhajan* developed within the *Bhakti* tradition, it has since been adopted by other Hindu traditions and even other religious groups.

The texts used in the devotional music (*bhajans* and *kirtans*) of the *Bhakti* Way in Hinduism are not identical to the Christian texts. The attitudes held by the Bhaktas, however, are very similar to those of Christians toward God. Communal celebrations with congregational singing are common to both. The Bhakti musical forms can be easily adapted for Christian worship by using texts with Christian interpretations. In relation to the form of *bhajan*, Fr. Amalorpavadass, founding director of the N.B.C.L.C. commented on their ability to create an atmosphere of recollection and to assist in the prayerfullness of the liturgy. It was his desire that all who listened to or participated in the singing of *bhajans* would attain an inner sense of peace. *Om Shanti*. [35] [36]

---

[35]"*Om*" contains the first, middle, and last letters of the *Devengari* alphabet. It is considered the primordial sound. It has much the same meaning of completeness as does the "A" and "Ω" of the Greek-speaking Christian Church. "*Shanti*" translates as "peace."

[36]Father. D. S. Amalorpavadass commentary on *Bhajans*. National Biblical, Catechetical and Liturgical Centre, *N.B.C.L.C. Bhajans Vol. 1A* (Bangalore, India: N.B.C.L.C.), side A.

CHAPTER 4
INDIAN PRAYER FORMS: *BHAJAN AND KIRTAN*

Two Indian forms of musical prayer have been adapted for use in Catholic worship with a great deal of success. These are *bhajan*, a type of antiphonal singing and *kirtan*, a type of congregational chant. Both have a long history within the *Bhakti* cults. Because they promote congregational singing and the full, conscious and active participation of the assembly,[37] they are quite useful in Catholic liturgy.

Bhajan a devotional song, hymn, or repetition of God's name.[38]

The *bhajan* is a choral form of music which developed in the communal worship of the Hindus within the *Bhakti* tradition. Essentially a *bhajan* is a "call and response" form of sung prayer. The leader (cantor) sings a simple phrase which is then repeated by (or acclaimed by) the rest of the community. This soloist/group dynamic is the primary characteristic of the form. Special care is taken in the composition of *bhajans* (whether set as compositions or improvised by the cantor) to include the assembly. Care is taken in the choice of melody and of text. A long text with a difficult melody would be disinviting for the assembly. Since most of the people in communities of the Hindu world were not trained in the intricacies of classical forms, the melodies which developed for bhajans are less complicated than the melodies of the classical Indian music. The *Bhakti* traditions in Southern India contain two principal formats for *bhajans*. Those known as *Thodaya Mangalam* present in a given order the songs attributed to particular Hindu saints from various regions. These *bhajans* use particular poetry, often grouped by language in an agreed upon order. This order takes the force of ritual in that it is always the same. The *bhajans* known as *Divyanama Bhajans* invoke God (*Brahma*) through the various manifestations (gods, goddesses) which have been a

---

[37]Flannery, p. 8.

[38]J.D. Choudhary, J.D., M.A. comp., *Concise Hindi-English Dictionary* (New Delhi, India: Kiran Publications), p. 524.

part of the lives and history of Hindus. While neither of these is textually appropriate for the Catholic liturgy, they may serve as general examples which may then be adapted to reflect Catholic theological understandings of God and appropriate reflections of this for liturgy.

Bhajans for the Catholic services may exist within several textual forms. In the simplest form, the cantor would sing a series of improvised phrases which the assembly would imitate. A litany form would be similar to the Hindu form of *Divyanama Bhajan*. Different litanies could be sung in this manner with the assembly either repeating the phrase as sung or singing an appropriate response. (This is actually an area of overlap because the Christian litanies already fulfill the requirements for this form of *bhajan*.) *Bhajans* could also be arranged which would follow particular patterned texts: these might include the *Stations of the Cross*, the *Mysteries of the Rosary*, the *Life of Christ*, and other patterned expressions of God's actions and salvation history. *Bhajans* might also be used which reflect particular actions in the liturgy. These might borrow texts from the antiphons provided by the liturgical documents. These would include *bhajans* based upon the *Introit Antiphons*, the *Communion Antiphons*, and the other antiphons which accompany the various Rites of the Church (such as the *Investiture Antiphon* from the *Rite of Ordination*). Since these antiphons do not require the use of a Psalm, the repetition of their text by the assembly in this format would be perfectly acceptable. *Bhajans* could also be used which would contain the texts of the *Invitatory Psalms*, the opening versicles for the *Liturgy of Hours* and other "set" liturgical texts. *Bhajans* may be set to familiar prayers which may then be sung by the assembly. There are also *bhajans* which are used in connection with particular liturgical actions such as the *dhuparati bhajans* celebrating the light as the Light of Christ. These *bhajans* would be used during the *lucernarium*, the ceremony of the lighting of the lamp.[39] Musical forms for *bhajans* may be divided into two convenient groupings. In the first, and most basic, the assembly repeats the same music and text that the cantor had sung. Whatever phrase the cantor sings, the assembly repeats. This is the most common form in Hindu *bhajans*. In the second, the cantor sings a list of phrases while the assembly answers by

---

[39]Sr. Jacinta, interviews by author, Tape recording, Bangalore, India, Summer 1990.

repeating a refrain or acclamation. This is the familiar pattern of a litany. Within these two groups there is much room for variation. The assembly might have a chorus which returns at a specific interval. The cantor (and/or assembly, and/or instrumentalists) might provide an introduction or a coda. Instrumental musicians may provide interludes between the verses of the *bhajan*. These might be simple short repetitions of previously given music, elaborations upon the melodies used, or contrasting musical themes from the same *raga* (Indian melodic formula). While the two fundamental forms appear simple, the musical variations allowed to the cantor and instrumentalists are numerous. The cantor may always choose to employ *gamaka* (graces) which are beyond the assembly's abilities. These graces (discussed later in more detail) are the very soul of Indian classical music. For that very reason, the assembly, which is not trained in their use, can not be expected to imitate them. When the cantor returns to a melody the second, third or fourth time, he or she may feel free to ornament it, while the assembly may respond with the simpler form. If some in the assembly respond with the same *gamaka* there will exist a type of heterophony which is very characteristic of Indian choral music. The solo/choral duality of *bhajans* allows the musicians a great deal of creativity in interpreting the texts without making the assembly's response overly difficult. Most *bhajans* employ simple but poetic texts which may be grasped easily yet meditated upon for long periods of time. In many ways *bhajans* are sung forms of *mantra*. (prayer using a repeated phrase)[40] An outline of the two basic forms with examples may be of value here.

1. Direct repetition. The cantor sings a phrase and the assembly repeats it, followed by the next phrase which is then repeated. Sometimes there are instrumental improvisations interspersed among the texts. This form takes the following characteristic pattern:

> (Introduction, Optional)
> A(Cantor)   A (Assembly)
> B(Cantor)   B (Assembly)
> (Instrumental Interlude, Optional)

---

[40]Sr. Jacinta, interviews by author, Tape recording, Bangalore, India, Summer 1990.

22

C(Cantor)   C (Assembly)
D(Cantor)   D (Assembly)
(Instrumental Interlude, Optional)
E(Cantor)   E (Assembly)
(Coda, Optional)

The music continues along this pattern, the same material may be used over and over again with or without subsequent changes in text. (Sometimes a single text is used and repeated over and over.)

An example of this type of *bhajan* is *Om Shanti* by Fr. Dr. Charles Vas, S.V.D. It includes an introduction, instrumental interludes, and a coda. Transliterations in the Roman alphabet and translations in English are provided below.

Om, Shanti

Om, Shanti, Om, Om, Shanti

Jan Lo Main Hoon Tumhara Ish, Main Hoon Tumhara Ish
Ji Prabhu Mann Liya Aap Mere Ish
Jan Lo Main Hoon Ish
Ji Prabhu Mann Liya Aap Mere Ish
Jan Lo Main Hoon Ish
Ji Prabhu Mann Liya Aap Mere Ish

Jan Lo Main Hoon Tumhara Nath, Main Hoon Tumhara Nath
Ji Prabhu Mann Liya Aap Mere Nath
Jan Lo Main Hoon Nath
Ji Prabhu Mann Liya Aap Mere Nath
Jan Lo Main Hoon Nath
Ji Prabhu Mann Liya Aap Mere Nath

Om Shanti, Om, Om, Shanti[41]

Om, Peace
Know my people that I am your God
Yes Lord! I believe that you are my God
Know my people that I am your Creator

---

[41] Copyright ©1989 Fr. Dr. Charles Vas, SVD, D.Mus. Used with permission. All rights reserved.

Yes Lord! I believe that you are my Creator[42]

2. Litany form. The cantor sings phrases which change while the community answers with a single acclamation. This is the same as the Christian litany, though there are more possible texts than there are in the traditional Christian litanies.

(Introduction, Optional))

A (Cantor)	X Response (Assembly)
B (Cantor)	X Response (Assembly)
C (Cantor)	X Response (Assembly)
D (Cantor)	X Response (Assembly)

(Coda, Optional)

---

[42]*N.B.C.L.C. Bhajans*, p. 11.

The music continues along this pattern; the same material may be used over and over again with the cantor providing more elaborate *gamaka* or other embellishments while the assembly maintains the simpler form of the phrase.

The following *bhajan* helps to illustrate this form. Most *bhajans* of this type are improvised and therefore, like much Indian music, they are not written down. A translation is provided for the transliterated text.

Jay dev

X Jay Dev Jay Dev Jay Dev X Jay Dev Jay Dev Jay Dev	Hail God. Hail God. Hail God. Hail God. Hail God. Hail God.
A 1 Jay Dev Jay Dev Jay Dev Pita Creator X Jay Dev Jay Dev Jay Dev	Hail God Hail God Hail God the Hail God. Hail God. Hail God.
B 2 Jay Dev He Putr Jay Dev Atma Spirit X Jay Dev Jay Dev Jay Dev	Hail God Oh! Son, Hail God the Hail God. Hail God. Hail God.
C 3 Jay Dev Jay Dev Jay srishtikarta	Hail God the Father
X Jay Dev Jay Dev Jay Dev	Hail God. Hail God. Hail God.
D 4 Jay manavoke tu utpanna karta	Hail to you origin of humanity
X Jay Dev Jay Dev Jay Dev	Hail God. Hail God. Hail God.
E 5 Jay Dev Jay Dev Jay Yesu Krista *Tujse tarna prapt hamko hai* *Samasta* X Jay Dev Jay Dev Jay Dev [43]	Hail God Hail God Hail Jesus Christ From whom we received redemption Hail God. Hail God. Hail God.

Many church musicians in India have come to experience *bhajans* as a marvelous tool for prayer in the liturgy. The dynamics of the form lead both the minister and those ministered to into deeper prayer. The form is unfamiliar to many of the Westernized Catholics in India, since the Church used Western music in the

---

[43]*N.B.C.L.C. Bhajans* #15, p. 6, adaptation by author.

Roman Rite and Syrian music in the Chaldeo-Indian Rites for centuries. Cultural Catholics had not been introduced to the *bhajan* form as the Church hierarchy had considered it Hindu. The Church had spent many years differentiating itself from Hinduism and Indian culture in general. Once many long-time Catholics have been initiated into *bhajan* singing, they often find this form most valuable in prayer. Some insight into this was provided by Sister Jacinta at the N.B.C.L.C. in Bangalore. She studied classical Indian music as well as classical Western music, but had not used classical Indian forms in prayer before coming to the N.B.C.L.C. She commented:

> I, myself, just started singing *[bhajans]*. I never had sung *bhajans* before, only the hymns of the vernacular tradition ... but after coming to the National Centre [N.B.C.L.C.] I am simply taken up by these *bhajans*. I have learned and I have performed [as a cantor] and I have sung in the groups ... I find it [a] quite meaningful, quite effective and prayerful form.[44]

Bhajans have become an integral part of the liturgical life of many Catholic Indians.

Namajapa

Namajapa from *Namah*, honorific greeting, and *Japa* which is to pray by repeating a phrase such as the name of the deity.[45]

One of the sub-groups within the *bhajan* form is worthy of particular note, *namajapa*. *Namajapa* is the ritual repetition of the Names (titles) of God. This is an ancient prayer form both in Hindu and in Christian tradition. The *Bhakti* movement also refers to the performance of *namajapa* as a form of *vandanam*, the chanting of the praise of God. The *bhaktas* spent many years in identifying and ritualizing the names of God. The *sadhasranama,* or thousand names of God, are numerous titles for *Brahma* which are chanted by the devotee.[46] The ideal is not that the devotee

[44]Sr. Jacinta, interview by author, Tape recording, Bangalore, India, 10 September 1990.

[45]J. D. Choudhary, pp. 278, 373.

[46]Father Anthony DeMello, S.J. *Sadhana A Way to God: Christian Excercises in Eastern Form*

should learn every possible title for God but rather seek the appropriate relationship with the eternal. "O my God, for you there are thousands of names, by which name should I call upon you?"[47]

Anjali Ashram, located near Mysore in Southern India, has written a *Namajapa* which they have titled *Namajapa: Invocation of the Nameless by Many Names.* The titles for God in this version are particularly Catholic in their imagery. This sort of adaptation of a Hindusthani form to a Catholic tradition seems particularly appropriate.[48]

The "Jesus Prayer" is an ancient Christian prayer form. In it the Christian is invited to repeat the name of Jesus over and over. The story of the Russian peasant[49] illustrates that this kind of prayer becomes a part of the rhythm of life for the devotee. Literally the prayer is inspired, breathed in and out. *Namajapa* does not have to be sung, but the control of the breath which occurs when singing the words is the same *yogic*[50] control desired by many. The body becomes one with the prayer. The tendency of persons while singing *namajapa* is to become silent. Each repetition is quieter until only the breathing is heard and silence has been attained. This is the silence of "Centering Prayer" as described by such prayer masters as Rev. Basil Pennington, O.C.S.O.[51]

Kirtan

Kirtan a musical recitation in praise of God.[52]

(Garden City, New York: Doubleday and Company, 1984), p. 117.

[47]Rev. Maurice D'Souza, C.S.C., notes from personal interviews.

[48]Anjali Ashram, "Namajapa: Invocation of the Nameless by Many Names" (Mysore, India) unpublished.

[49]*The Way of a Pilgrim*, trans. R. M. French (New York: Ballantine Books, 1974.)

[50]Control of the body as practiced in the various forms of *yoga*.

[51]See Abbot Thomas Keating O.S.C.O., M. Basil Pennington, O.S.C.O., and Thomas E. Clarke, S.J. *Finding Grace at the Center* (Still River, Massachusetts: St. Bede Publications, 1977).

[52]J. D. Choudhary p. 158.

Kirtan is a form of ritual music from the Hindu tradition which closely resembles Christian hymnody. A text which praises God is sung or proclaimed with musical accompaniment. The simple three-toned recitation resembles the reciting-tones of the Catholic Church both in its Latin and Syrian Rites.

Another important use for *kirtan* is in the ritual acclamations of texts. For this use there is no cantor/assembly dialogue. Instead, the entire assembly sings the text together. All of the acclamations for the Ordinary of the Mass fall into this category (the *Kyrie, Gloria, Alleluia/ Tractus, Sanctus, Mysterium Fidei, Amen,* and the *Agnus Dei*). There are other phrases in the Proper which may also be set in this manner. One important phrase which exemplifies this form is the following Sanskrit prayer:

Asato ma sad gamaya	From the unreal lead me to the real
Tamaso ma jyotir gamaya	From darkness lead me to the light
Mrityor ma amritam gamaya	From death lead me to immortality
Om shanti, shanti, shanti.	*Om*, Peace.[53]

It is worth noting that the principal difference between a Western setting of the acclamations and an indigenized Indian setting is not found in the form itself, but in the use of the Indian *ragas* (melodic modes/melody fragments each with its own emotional content) and *talas* (rhythmic modes). Even while using the *ragas*, it may be difficult for the Western ear to hear a difference between Indian and Western settings since six of the ten *thatts* (the fundamental modes which underlie all *ragas*) are identical with Western modes. The difference between *kirtan* and song may remain a point of interest only for musicologists. To understand the fullness of *ragas* is to begin to realize the essence of indigenization in the liturgy. While it is possible to enjoy Indian music and to be very involved in the assembly's song without understanding the subtleties of Indian music, the true depth of the music of India requires an understanding of the nuances of this musical language in all its richness.

---

[53]*N.B.C.L.C. Bhajans.* p. 87.

CHAPTER 5
ON *RAGAS* AND *RASAS*

Classical Indian music exists in two primary and related forms. In the Dravidian South, Karnatic Classical music theory is practiced while in the North, Hindusthani classical theory is used. For consistency this paper will deal in Hindusthani terms even though there are corresponding terms for use in Karnatic music. The two divisions are closely related both in history and in theory, much as French Classical music is related to Italian Classical music. In both systems, the principal organizing factor is the use of *ragas*. A *raga* is in effect a melodic formula, the seeds of an idea which may be expanded upon by the musician. Each *raga* has a *rasa* or specific emotional connotation (it may seem a denotation to Western ears). Some *ragas* are mournful, others joyous. Each has its place and use which should not be violated.

There are a number of defining factors involved for a grouping of notes to be recognizable as a *raga*. The *raga* is derived from a scale (more precisely a mode known as a *thatt* or *mela*). The notes which are used in the *raga* will be selected from the basic group of *thatts*, such as the ten suggested by Pandit Bhatkhande.[54]

Each *raga* contains two pivotal notes in addition to the universal tonic. The *vadi* (that which sounds)[55] may be considered the "King" of the *raga*. All the notes of the *raga* will gravitate towards this one (which may or may not be the tonic of the mode). The second axial note upon which the *raga* turns is the *samvadi* (always a fifth above or below the *vadi*). This second center may be considered the "minister" to the king of the *raga*. [56]

---

[54]Pandit Bhatkande was probably the most influential Hindusthani music theorist of the twentieth century. Even those who disagree with his theories must do so using the standardized terms he established.

[55]B. Chaintanya Deva, *Indian Music* (New Delhi, India: Indian Council for Cultural Relations, 1974), p. 15.

[56]B. Chaintanya Deva, p. 15.

The principal patterns which define the *raga* in Hindusthani music include an ordered ascent and descent. The order of ascent (*aroha*) and descent (*avroha*) for each *raga* are documented for all Hindusthani *ragas.*[57] A characteristic phrase known as the *pakad* is also recorded for each *raga*. It serves as identification for the listener; it is the basic touch of the *raga*.

The Indian octave (*saptak*) contains seven notes (*swaras*). A *raga* must contain at least five *swaras*. Each *swara* in the scale has a name and the first letter of that name is used when singing the Indian version of *solfeggio*. The names come from the ancient secular music theorists of Hindusthan. While the Hindusthani system is a movable one, it is useful to represent the Indian notes by using the "C" scale of Western music to represent the *shuddha* (pure) *swaras* of the Indian *ragas* (see Figure 1: India *Solfeggio*).

Shadaj	(C)	Sa
Rishabha	(D)	Ri
Gandhar	(E)	Ga
Maddhyam	(F)	Ma
Pancham	(G)	Pa
Dhavat	(A)	Dha
Nishad	(B)	Ni

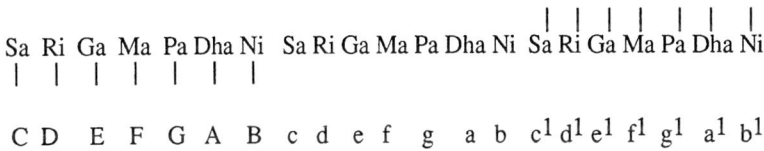

```
                                    |  |  |  |  |  |  |
Sa Ri Ga Ma Pa Dha Ni  Sa Ri Ga Ma Pa Dha Ni  Sa Ri Ga Ma Pa Dha Ni
|  |  |  |  |  |  |

C  D   E  F  G  A  B   c  d   e   f   g    a  b   c¹ d¹ e¹ f¹ g¹ a¹ b¹
```

Figure 1: India *Solfeggio*

There are three principal *saptaks*: the middle *saptak* (*madhya sthayi*), the higher *saptak* (*tara sthayi*), and the lower *saptak* (*mandra sthayi*). It is possible to expand this by adding other *sthayis* progressively higher and lower.

---

[57]Karnatic *ragas* also include divisions of ascent and descent, but a more limited number than the Hindusthani. For the Karnatic the ascent is either straight or crooked. Two *ragas* in Hindusthani music may have all of the same notes with one *raga* emphasizing one pitch while the other *ragas* stresses another; the Karnatic musician would say they were different uses of the same *raga*.

It is important to know that there is no established reference pitch in Indian music. The tonic note, *Sa*, may be placed wherever the singer or instrumentalist desires. (This is similar to the "movable Do" *solfeggio* used in Western music.) Hindusthani theory recognizes the seven natural (*shuddha*) notes as listed above. It also recognize five altered notes (*vikrita*). It does not use enharmonic notations. There are four "flat" notes which are referred to as *komal* , which can mean "tender."[58] These are *Ri komal* (Db), *Ga komal* (Eb), *Dha komal* (Ab), and *Ni komal* (Bb). There is a single "sharp" note called *teevra* (strong); it is *Ma teevra* (F#). With its seven *shuddha* notes and the five *vikrita* notes, Hindusthani theory can be represented by using western notation. There is a problem with this in that each of the *vikrita* notes has several variants. The *Vikrita Ma* (F) may be sharp (*teevra*) or middle sharp (*madhya teevra*), or exceedingly sharp (*ateeteevra*). The *vikrita* of the *komal* notes (D, E, A, and B) may be flat (*komal*), middle flat (*madhya komal*), or exceedingly flat (*ateekomal*). The generally accepted number of *sruti* (notes which may be distinguished)[59] in the Hindusthani octave is actually twenty-two. These are not equal subdivisions and, therefore, they cannot be transposed without the re-tuning of each accompanying instrument.

The reason for this strangely ordered division is not difficult to grasp. Until the Middle Ages, Hindusthani (and presumably Karnatic) music was based on a Pythagorean mathematical scale. This scale of seven *shuddha* notes is very close to the untempered Western Diatonic scale. The various modes were exactly that -- modes. The tonic would be shifted while maintaining the same absolute pitches for each *swara*. These various combinations of whole and half steps in mathematical tunings were arrived at by using *moorchana paddhati* (modal shift). Sometime during the fifteenth century, Indian musicians began to shift the tonic notes of the

---

[58] Arthur Henry Fox-Strangeways, *The Music of Hindostan*, (Oxford: Clarendon Press, 1914; reprint, Oxford: University Press, 1967).

[59] *Sruti* may be rendered as "to hear" or as "that which is heard." Musically the term is used to refer to the interval between notes which can be distinguished aurally. There is an almost limitless number of pitches which may be used, but twenty-two unequal divisions are the heritage of the Hindusthani musicians. The division into twenty two *sruti* (segments) does not imply any equality in since there is no equal temperament involved in Indian music theory. Notes from Fr. Dr. Charles Vas, S.V.D. by the author, Summer 1990.

modes so that they used a single tonic. This allows a musician to sing any *raga* in his or her best possible range. The accompanying instrument(s) did not have to be re-tuned to the new tonic note. Because the tunings were mathematical rather than tempered, the transposed *moorchana* (modes) do not use the same absolute pitches. The *vikrita* notes exist in three variations and Indian musicians maintain these differences to the present day.

Time and Raga

In Hindusthani music, each *raga* is used during a particular time of the day. The cycle of the day is divided into eight *prahara*s (watches) each of which lasts for three hours. There is a complex relationship between *ragas* and time. It may help to understand a simplification of this cycle as diagrammed below:

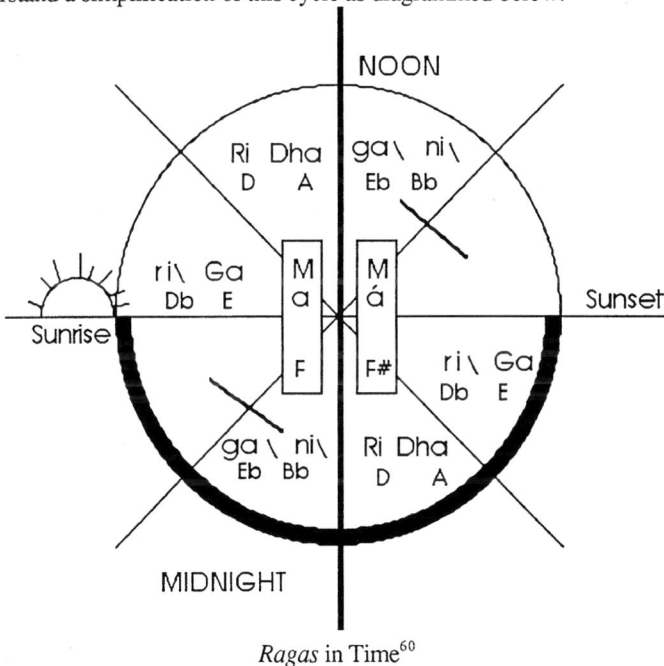

Ragas in Time[60]

Figure 2: Time and Raga

---

[60]Author's notes from studies with Dr. Charles Vas, SVD, D.Mus.

The Ten *Thatts* of *Pandit* Bhatkhande
with associated *Ragas* for *Bhajans*

Pandit Bhatkhande was an early twentieth-century music theorist from what is now the state of Maharastra. He proposed the following set of ten basic modes (*thatts*) from which all *ragas* could be derived. He named these *thatts* with the names of well-known *ragas* which used these notes. While this system is not nearly as mathematically complete as the Karnatic system, it is very useful for discussing Indian music in Western terms. It is easily represented in Western notation. It may help to look at these *thatts* (and some of the *ragas* based upon them) in the order they are presented by *Pandit* Bhatkhande. The following *Ragas* and *Thatts* are presented in the form presented by *Sangeet Abhinay* Academy in Bandra, Bombay, India.

Kalyan Thatt

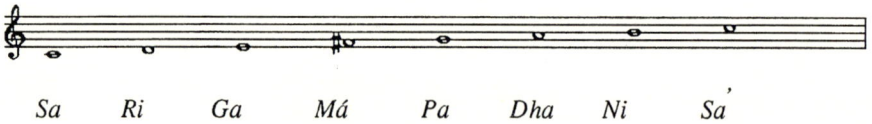

| Sa | Ri | Ga | Má | Pa | Dha | Ni | Sa' |

Example 1: *Kalyan Thatt*

Kalyan Thatt corresponds very closely to the *Lydian* Mode in Western music. The *ragas* based upon this *thatt* are usually reserved for use after sunset.

Raga Kalyan (Kalyan Thatt)

Raga Kalyan is characterized by its use of the raised fourth scale degree, *Ma teevra*. This raga is usually used in the first part of the night. The *rasa* of this *raga* is loving.

The ascending order (*aroha*) is straightforward and includes all seven *swaras* making this a *sampurna raga*. Likewise the descending order (*avroha*) includes all seven *swaras* and is straightforward. The characteristic phrase (*pakad*) begins on the seventh scale step (*Ni*) which is the *samvadi*. *Ga*, the *vadi*, is also emphasized in the *pakad* in that it is held for a longer period of time than the other notes. The accompanying *tambura* [61] would be tuned to *Sa, Pa, Sa^y, Sa^y*. The sounding of *Sa* and *Ni* together at the beginning of a phrase is considered by many Indian musicians to be delightful and restful. As in all *ragas*, the final resolution is to the tonic note, *Sa*.[62]

Example 2: *Raga Kalyan*

Bilaval Thatt

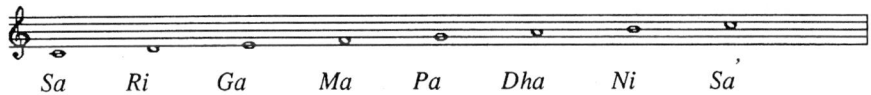

Sa	Ri	Ga	Ma	Pa	Dha	Ni	Sa

Example 3: *Bilaval Thatt*

---

[61] The *tambura* is a stringed instrument which is used in accompanying both instrumental and vocal music. It consists of a large gourd with a long neck added. Four strings are placed on this three of which are tuned to various *saptaks* of *Sa*. The other string is usually tuned to *Pa*, but when *Pa* is *varj* (absent) it may be tuned to *Ma*. If both *Pa* and *Ma* are *varj*, this string is not plucked. The instrument provides a constant drone with no attention paid to the rhythm of the music. A steady solid drone is preferable.

[62] Author's notes, studies with Fr. Dr. Charles Vas, S.V.D., D.Mus. at *Sangeet Abhinay* Academy, Bandra, 7 August, 1990. p. 23.

[63] Author's notes, studies with Fr. Dr. Charles Vas, S.V.D., D.Mus. "Notebook A," p. 23, "Notebook B," p. 16.

Bilaval thatt corresponds almost exactly to the Western diatonic major scale (some pitches are slightly different because it is a mathematical and not a tempered scale). It contains only *shuddha swaras* (unaltered notes). The *ragas* based upon this *thatt* are usually reserved for use in the morning. *Ragas* which are often used in *bhajans* which belong to this family include: *Raga Bilaval, Raga Bhupali,* and *Raga Jansamohini.*

Raga Bilaval (Bilaval Thatt)

Raga Bilaval corresponds with the Western major diatonic scale. It contains only *shuddha* (pure) *swaras. Ni* (B) is used only as a grace note (*andolan* or *gamaka*) resolving down to *Dha* (A). The *aroha* is pentatonic (excluding *Ma* and *Ni*, except as *gamaka*); the *avroha* is hexatonic in that it excludes only *Ni.* This *raga* mixes expressions of joy, affection, tenderness and activity. It may reflect many moods.

The *aroha* is pentatonic with straightforward motion except for the *gamaka.* The *avroha* is *vakra* (crooked) and heptatonic. The *pakad* begins on Dha (A) which is the *vadi. Ga,* the sam*vadi,* is also emphasized in the *pakad* in that it is held for a longer period of time than the other notes. It may be useful to note that while the scale appears to be the same as the Western Major scale, the use is different. *Ma* (F) is never used in ascending and the accompaniment would yield a minor chord (C-tonic, A-*vadi*, E-*samvadi*).

Example 4: *Raga Bilaval*

---

[64]Author's notes, "Notebook A," pp. 23-23b, "Notebook B," p. 15.

Raga Bhupali (Bilaval Thatt)

Raga Bhupali also corresponds with the Western major diatonic scale. *Ma* and *Ni* are *varj* (absent) making this *raga* pentatonic both in ascent and in descent. This *raga* has the same characteristics as the Pythagorean pentatonic scale which is used in China and Tibet. It occurs in the second part of the night. *Raga Bhupali* is characterized by emotions of saintly detachment, confidence, self-reliance, all in the tenderness of the night.

Note the characteristic *andolan* (type of grace note) which goes from *Sa* down to *Dha* and returns to *Sa*. The *pakad* begins on Ga (E) which is the *vadi*. *Ri*, the *Nyas* (note which is held) is also emphasized in the *pakad*.

Example 5: *Raga Bhupali*

Raga Jansamohini (Bilaval Thatt)

Raga Jansamohini is created by adding *Ni* (B) to *Raga Bhupali*.

Example 6: *Raga Jansamohini*

---

[65]Author's notes, "Notebook A," pp. 4, "Notebook B," p. 1.

[66]Author's notes, "Notebook A," pp. 14, "Notebook B," p. 9.

Khamaj Thatt

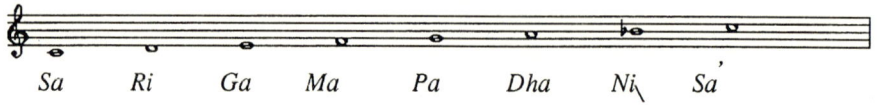

Sa   Ri   Ga   Ma   Pa   Dha   Ni   Sa

Example 7: *Khamaj Thatt*

Khamaj Thatt contains the same *swaras* as the Western *Mixolydian* mode. Most of the *ragas* based on this *thatt* are used in the evening. They would be useful for the *Liturgy of the Hours* in *Evening Prayer*. *Ragas* which are based on *Khamaj Thatt* include: *Raga Khamaj* and *Raga Kalawati*.

Raga Khamaj (Khamaj Thatt)

Raga Khamaj corresponds with the Western major diatonic scale while ascending and with the Mixolydian mode while descending. This *raga* expresses the tender memories of joy, contentment, hope and desire.

The *aroha* is heptatonic with a straightforward ascent (not *vakra*) and uses only *shuddha* (pure) *swaras* (notes). The *avroha* is also straightforward, but uses *Ni komal* (Bb). The *pakad* begins on the *vadi, Ga* and returns to it. The final cadence would still be to the tonic, *Sa*. The *samvadi* is *Ni komal*, which is not allowed to resolve upward to *Sa*; It is only allowed to resolve down to *Dha*. *Ni shuddha* resolves upward to *Sa*.

Example 8: *Raga Khamaj*

---

[67] Author's notes, "Notebook A," pp. 20-3, "Notebook B," p. 14.

Raga Kalawati (Khamaj Thatt)

Raga Kalawati is a *Karnatic raga* which has been borrowed and used throughout India. It is particularly popular for use in *bhajan* singing. The *aroha* is pentatonic, with *Ni komal* never resolving to *Sa*. This gives a very clear under-third cadence. Likewise the *avroha* is also pentatonic and also *vakra*. Again notice the under-third cadence. The *Pakad* begins on the *Nyas* (*Ga*) and ascends to *Ni komal*. From this point it is identical with the *Avroha*. The *Vadi* is *Pa* while the *samvadi* is *Sa* (also tonic). The three emphasized notes create a major tonic chord which may help explain this *raga's* appeal to Western ears.

Example 9: *Raga Kalawati*

Bhairav Thatt

| Sa | Ri | Ga | Ma | Pa | Dha | Ni | Sa |

Example 10: *Bhairav Thatt*

Bhairav Thatt has no Western equivalent. It includes a flat second scale step as well as a flat sixth scale step. The pattern "*Ga* (E), *Ri komal* (Db), *Sa* (C)" can not be developed in Western modes, but could be developed by using modal shift of the Western Harmonic Minor. This *thatt* belongs to the *Ma gramma* which Western

---

[68] Author's notes, "Notebook A," pp. 17-8, "Notebook B," p. 11.

music does not use.[69] It is used primarily in the early morning, at sunrise. It is a family of ragas belonging to the morning twilight.

Raga Bhairav (Bhairav Thatt)

Raga Bhairav is very popular for use in *bhajan* singing. *Bhairav Thatt* is the basis for many of the *ragas* used for *bhajans*. This *raga* is *vakra* both in ascent and in descent and had a lowered second scale step (*Ri komal*) as well as a lowered sixth scale step (*Dha komal*). It is a strong and popular *raga* and has been so through the centuries.

The *andolan* (graces) on *Dha komal* and *Ri komal* are very important. Notice that they are used in the *aroha*, the *avroha* and the *pakad*. The *pakad* begins on *Ga* and quickly turns into the same phrase as the *avroha*. The *Vadi, Dha komal,* and the *samvadi, Ri komal,* are emphasized both by repetition and by ornamentation (*andolan*).

Example 11: *Raga Bhairav*

Raga Jyogi (Bhairav Thatt)

Raga Jyogi is very devotional and is popular for us in *bhajans* which relate to sad emotions such as longing or mourning. It is very appropriate for use when texts

---

[69]The *Sa Gramma* (*gamut*) is the pattern which yields the Western modes (and their related Indian counterparts). The *Ma gramma* which is not commonly used in the West includes an "augmented second." It is used in Middle-Eastern and Eastern European music.

[70]Author's notes, "Notebook A," pp. 23-4, "Notebook B," p. 4.

refer to the longing of humanity for God. The expression is often of one half-asleep and disturbed.

Notice that the *raga* is pentatonic in ascent and heptatonic in descent. The *andolan* on *Dha komal* and *Ri komal* are very important. The Major third - minor second - tonic pattern which resolves the *avroha* is very characteristic of this *raga*. *Ga* is never used by itself in this *raga*; it always resolves to *Ri komal*. The first *pakad* begins on *Ma* and emphasizes the *andolan* on *Ri komal*. The alternate *pakad* begins on *Sa* following basically the *Aroha* and *avroha*. *Ma* is the *vadi* while *Sa* serves as both *samvadi* and tonic.

Example 12: *Raga Jyogi*

Poorvi Thatt

Example 13: *Poorvi Thatt*

Poorvi Thatt also has no Western equivalent. It contains *Ri komal* (Db), *Ma shuddha* (F "pure"), *Ma teevra* (F#), and *Dha komal* (Db). The *ragas* based upon this *thatt* are very difficult to sing and they are seldom if ever used for the

---

[71] Author's notes, "Notebook A," pp. 39-40, "Notebook B," p. 23b.

composition of *bhajans*. These *ragas* are primarily used by classical singers and are usually performed in the evening twilight.

Raga Poorvi (Poorvi Thatt)

Raga Poorvi, according to Fr. Dr. Charles Vas, S.V.D., D. Mus., includes *Ri komal, Ma, Ma Teevra,* and *Dha komal. Ma teevra* is only used while ascending. (*Puravi* [sic], according to Alain Daniélou, includes *Dha shuddha* instead of *Dha komal,* with the rest of the *swaras* remaining the same.) The emotional context is one of prayer and petition. It is associated with sunset and the twilight time when humanity dreams. Using both *Ma shuddha* and *Ma teevra* is said to give energetic expression and signifies happiness. The *Ri komal* is said to be a tender and touching *swara.*

The *aroha* and *avroha* are both heptatonic, making this a *sampurna raga.* One very important phrase is found both in the *avroha* and the *pakad: Pa, Ma teevra, Ga, Ma shuddha, Ga, Ri komal, Ma shuddha, Ga, Ma teevra, Ri komal, Sa.* This particular pattern is very difficult to sing with correct pitching of each note. This *raga* is usually reserved for use by well-trained singers and is seldom used for *bhajans.* The *pakad* begins on *Dha komal* and proceeds with the pattern mentioned above. This pattern, like the features of a person's face, is recognizable. In Hindi the word used is *sakal* which means "the face."[72] It is incumbent on the musician to bring out the face of the *raga.* The *vadi* is *Ga* and the *samvadi* is *Ni.*

Example 14: *Raga Poorvi*

---

[72]B. Chaintanya Deva, p.12.

[73]Author's notes, "Notebook A," pp. 29-30, "Notebook B," p. 21.

Marva Thatt

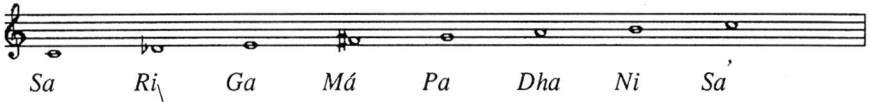

Sa   Ri   Ga   Má   Pa   Dha   Ni   Sa

Example 15: *Marva Thatt*

Marva thatt also has no Western equivalent. It is almost as difficult to sing as *Poorvi Thatt*. The *ragas* based on this *thatt* are usually reserved for use during the hours of the evening twilight.

Raga Marva (Marva Thatt)

Raga Marva is hexatonic (*shadava*) since *Pa* is *varj*. It may be best characterized by this lack of the fifth scale step. It leaves the *raga* missing something. It gives it a certain feel of uneasiness and expectation. Somewhat violent in connotation, this *raga* may also be rendered using the tender *Ri komal*. It is a rough and unfinished *raga* sung before the sunset.

Raga Marva is often developed in the higher *saptak*. The *Sa* of the second *saptak* is avoided as noted below in the *aroha* and *avroha*. This is a difficult *raga* to sing and is usually reserved for use in classical singing rather than in devotional songs. The *pakad* begins on the tender *swara, Ri komal*. It studiously avoids the sounding of the tonic *Sa* until the final resolution. Played without the accompaniment, this *raga* may seem very strange. When the accompanying *Sa* and *Pa* are sounded on *tambura*, the *pakad* takes on an entirely different character. The *vadi* is *Dha* and the *samvadi, Ri komal*, is much stressed. This is a difficult *raga* which may be used effectively by a soloist, but it is seldom used by an assembly for common prayer.

Example 16: *Raga Marva*

Kafi Thatt

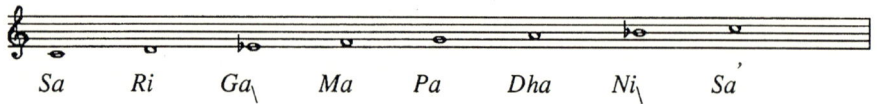

| Sa | Ri | Ga\ | Ma | Pa | Dha | Ni\ | Sa' |

Example 17: *Kafi Thatt*

Kafi Thatt corresponds to the Western Dorian mode. The *ragas* based on this *thatt* are very popular for use in *bhajans*. Most of these *ragas* are used in the nighttime, that is, after sundown. They would be appropriate for use with *Night Prayer* in the *Liturgy of the Hours*. They include: *Raga Kafi* as well as *Raga Mishra* (mixed) *Kafi*, which may use *Ga* and *Ni Shuddha*. in addition to *Ga* and *Ni komal*.

Raga Kafi (Kafi Thatt)

Raga Kafi is light and gentle. It is not considered to have great depth of emotion. It is traditionally used for *thappa* (songs of the desert camel drovers of Rajasthan), *bhajans* and the *hori* festival (where everyone throws colored powders on each other). It is a pleasant and peaceful *raga*.

Raga Kafi is very popular and simple to sing. It is heptatonic (*sampurna*) and consistent. It occurs during the second quarter of the night. Some authorities claim that the *vadi* is *Pa*, the *samvadi* is *Sa* and *Ri* is used as *Nyas*. (Others believe that *Ri* is actually the *samvadi*.) The *pakad* begins on the vadi and includes the very

---

[74] Author's notes, "Notebook A," pp. 27-8, "Notebook B," p. 20.

characteristic phrase: *Pa, Ma, Ga komal, Ri.* This *raga* is often used by groups in common both for *bhajans* and for *kirtan.*

Example 18: *Raga Kafi*

Asavari Thatt

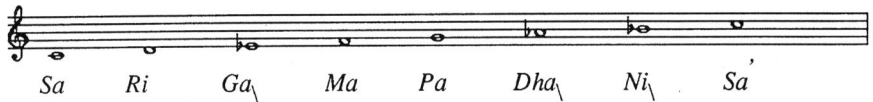

Sa   Ri   Ga\   Ma   Pa   Dha\   Ni\   Sa'

Example 19: *Asavari Thatt*

Asavari Thatt (sometimes known as *Yavanapuri*) contains the same notes as the Western Natural Minor Scale. The *ragas* based on this *thatt* are very popular for *bhajans.* This family of *ragas* has a familiar ring to Western ears. The chant-like settings of the *bhajan*, coupled with the familiar-sounding mode, may lead the Western listener to believe this music is not Indian. Many Western musicians are drawn to this *thatt* when they begin to study Indian music because it is so similar to the material they already know. *Ragas* in this family include: *Raga Asavari, Raga Malkauns,* and *Raga Darbari Kanada.*

Raga Asavari (Asavari Thatt)

Raga Asavari is characterized as tender and loving with grace and beauty. This *raga* is referred to in many ancient texts as *Raga Yavanapuri*, which is considered a

---

[75]Author's notes, "Notebook A," pp. 24, "Notebook B," p. 18.

combination of features selected from *Raga Deshi* and *Raga Gandhari*. Pandit Bhatkhande chose to refer to this as a *thatt*, and assigned to it the name *Asavari*.[76]

Raga Asavari is hexatonic in ascent; *Ga komal* is *varj*. The *aroha* exemplifies the *raga* in particular by the repetition of the *andolan* on *Dha komal*. The *Avroha* includes a relatively fast section of written *gamaka* ending on *Pa* and a repeated *andolan* on *Ga komal*. The *pakad* is identical with the second half of the *avroha*. An alteration is allowed during faster developments (*tan*); *Ni komal* may be used while ascending in fast development. The phrase "*Ma, Pa, Dha komal, Ma, Pa--, Ga komal, Ri, Sa*" is used to differentiate this *raga* from *Dharbari Kanada*. The *vadi* is *Dha komal* and the *samvadi* is *Ga komal*.

Example 20 *Raga Asavari*

Raga Malkauns (Asavari Thatt)

Raga Malkauns is a pentatonic *raga* which leaves *Ri* and *Pa varj*. It is usually performed in the morning twilight and has conotations of deep peace and abandonment in the peace of the night.

This *raga* is *vakra* while ascending and straightforward while descending. It is considered very consonant by many Indian musicians and therefore peaceful. One may note that there are no half step relationships in this *raga*. The *pakad* begins on *Dha komal* of the *mandra sthayi* (lower *saptak*). The *vadi, Ma,* is highly

---

[76]According to many Sanskrit texts, *Raga Asavari* contains *Ri komal, Ga komal, Dha komal* and *Ni Komal*. This *Raga Asavari* is not one of Bhatkhande's *thatts*, and it would be considered a *raga* from his *Bhairavi Thatt*. More information on this *raga* is available in Daniélou, pp. 164-166.

[77]Author's notes, "Notebook A," pp. 25, 26, "Notebook B," p.19.

emphasized while the *samvadi, Sa,* is also the tonic. In this *raga* the *tambura* would be tuned to *Sa* and *Ma* since *Pa* is *varj* (absent).

Example 21: *Raga Malkauns*

Raga Darbari Kanada (Asavari Thatt)

Raga Darbari Kanada is a *Karnatic raga* which has become popular throughout India. It is particularly useful for *bhajan* singing. It is developed in the middle and lower *saptaks.* This *raga* is characterized by great solemnity and deep emotion.

This *raga* belongs to the quiet of the night. There is special stress given to the *swaras Ga komal, Dha komal* and *Ni komal.* These stresses take the form of *andolan* in the *avroha.* One may notice the great stresses laid upon these notes even though they are not the axial notes of the *raga.* The *avroha* is *vakra* with great stress laid upon *Pa,* the *samvadi.* in the second half of the *avroha* the *vadi, Ri,* is emphasized with a written *gamaka.* This written *gamaka* is very characteristic of the *raga.* The *pakad* begins on *Ni komal* of the *mandra sthayi* (lower *saptak*) . It emphasizes the *vadi* and the tonic in the first half, but descends to emphasize the *samvadi* in the second half. It may be important to note that this will change the register in which the singer(s) sings and will invariably result in a darker tone color. Because of the solemnity of this *raga* it is usually developed slowly with great dignity.

---

[78]Author's notes, "Notebook A," pp. 6, 7, "Notebook B," p. 2.

46

Example 22: *Raga Darbari Kanada*

Bhairavi Thatt

Sa   Ri   Ga   Ma   Pa   Dha   Ni   Sa

Example 23: *Bhairavi Thatt*

Bhairavi Thatt contains the same notes as the Western Phrygian Mode. It uses all four *komal swaras: Ri komal*(Db), *Ga komal*(Eb), *Dha komal* (Ab), and *Ni komal* (Bb). This *Ri komal* is very low, with a strong tendency to *Sa*. The *ragas* of this family belong primarily to the morning and are very popular for use in *bhajan* singing. They include: *Raga Bhairavi, Raga Mishra Bhairavi* (which uses *Ri shuddha* in addition to *Ri komal*), and *Raga Bilaskhani Todi* which uses the notes of *Bhairavi Thatt* but the *pakad* of *Raga Todi.*

Raga Bhairavi (Bhairavi Thatt)

Raga Bhairavi is a heptatonic *raga* which is characterized as being very tender, loving and yet sad. There is a feeling of melancholy associated with this *raga*. It is usually performed in the late morning (before noon) and is popular for use in

---

[79]Author's notes, "Notebook A," pp. 15, 16, "Notebook B," p. 10.

bhajan and *kirtan* singing. It may be modified by adding *Ri shuddha* and/or *Ma Teevra* to create *Mishra* (mixed) *Bhairavi*.

This is a melodious *raga* with two choices for *samvadi*. It may be taken as *Pa* which is considered the more devotional or as *Ma* which is considered the more somber. The *pakad* is simple and direct and ends with a very characteristic *Sa, Ri komal, Sa* pattern.

Example 24: *Raga Bhairavi*

The following phrase is characteristic of the *Mishra* form, though the *pakad* does not show the additional use of *Ma teevra*.

Example 25: *Raga Mishra Bhairavi*

Raga Bilaskhani Todi (Bhairavi Thatt)

Raga Bilaskhani Todi was developed by Bilas Khan, who was the son of the great Medieval musician and theorist Tan Sen. This *raga* uses the notes of *Raga Bharavi*, but ends with the characteristic phrase of *Raga Todi* (see below). This is a very devotional *raga* which is often used in the singing of *bhajans* and *kirtan*. It belongs to the morning; some writers place it early in the morning while others

---

[80]Author's notes, "Notebook A," pp. 12, 13, 25, "Notebook B," p. 17.

place it later in the morning. The Sanskrit poetic texts were composed by Hindu Scholars and musicians during the Vedic period. There is no Sanskrit text describing this *raga* since Bilas Khan served the court of the great Moghul emperor much later during the medieval period. A Muslim musician working in the court of the greatest of Muslim rulers in India would not compose a Hindu/Sanskrit text about the *raga*.

Some writers consider this *raga* to belong to *Todi Thatt* while other (notably Bhatkhande) assigns it to *Bhairavi Thatt* because of the notes it contains.[81] The *pakad* ends with the same phrase as does *Raga Todi*. The *vadi* is *Dha komal* and the *samvadi* is *Gha komal*. *Ri komal* also seems to be stressed, though theorists have not marked it as *Nyas*.

Example 26: *Raga Bilaskhani Todi*

Todi Thatt

Example 27: *Todi Thatt*

Todi Thatt is unlike any Western mode. It contains *Ri komal* (Db), *Ga komal* (Eb), *Dha komal* (Ab), and *Ma teevra* (F#). Some of the *ragas* of this family are characterized as morning *ragas*, while others are considered to belong to the

---

[81]Daniélou, pp. 148-150.

[82]Author's notes, "Notebook A," pp. 33-34, "Notebook B," p. 23.

evening. When a *raga* contains *Ma teevra*, the *raga* is usually considered an evening *raga* (as explained below), but many of these *ragas* (including *Raga Todi* itself) do not emphasize *Ma teevra* at all. These are surprisingly classified as morning *Ragas* even though they contain *Ma teevra*. This is allowed because they use it only in *gamaka*.

Raga Todi (Todi Thatt)

Raga Todi is considered a morning *raga* because *Ri komal* is not stressed and *Ma teevra* is seldom used. It is considered an attractive *raga* and is said to contain the emotions of sadness, tenderness, love, mixed to some degree with vanity and sternness.

The *pakad* begins by emphasizing Ni and Ga komal and ends with the characteristic *Ri komal, Ga komal, Ri komal, Sa* pattern. This is called the "*Todi* touch" and is found in the *raga Todi* above.

Example 28: *Raga Todi*

---

[83] Author's notes, "Notebook A," pp. 31-2, "Notebook B," p. 22.

CHAPTER 6

ON RHYTHM AND *TALAS*

A complete understanding of the functions of tempo and rhythm in Indian music is far beyond the scope of this work. A short introduction to the uses of *talas* (rhythm patterns) is required for the understanding of their use in *bhajans*.

Indian music recognizes three basic tempos (*laya*). Each is related to the others by being approximately twice as fast as the preceding tempo. The slowest tempo is called *vilambit*; it is usually reserved for dignified music and is often the tempo of temple music. In *vilambit* tempos each beat (*matra*) lasts approximately one second
(60mm). The second tempo is known as *madhyam* or medium. In this tempo one *matra* tends to last only half a second (120mm) It is a very popular tempo for *bhajan* singing. The fastest tempo is *drut*. The *drut* tempo is quite popular for light songs and work songs. At this tempo the *matra* lasts about a quarter of one second (240mm). Sometimes a *bhajan* is begun in one tempo and switched by the cantor to a higher tempo. The tempo later reverts to the slower. Most *bhajans* would not be begun in *drut* fashion, but many will spend time in it.[84]

Regularly recurring cyclic rhythm patterns are used to organize most Indian music. These patterns are called *talas*. A *tala* can be several measures long according to Western understanding and may include several different meters.

In each cycle there are three basic parts: the *sama* is the principal or heavy beat; the *kali* is an "empty beat" or rest; and other beats each of which is called *tali*.

Most Hindusthani music is accompanied by *tabla*. *Tabla* refers to a set of two small drums: the *dagga* and the *dyan* (also called *tabla*). Both of these are played by a single person. The *dagga* (left hand drum) is a kettle-shaped instrument of metal or pottery roughly ten inches tall with a center diameter also of about ten

---

[84]Author's notes, "Notebook B," p. 46.

inches. The head is made with two pieces of leather. The first is what most Western musicians would recognize as a head; the second is a collar which surrounds the first while both are bound to the drum. Slightly off the center of the head is a load made of some form of paste. This drum is tuned with itself only and is capable of great variation in pitch. The *dyan* (right hand drum) is a cylindrical instrument made of wood. Its head is constructed in the same manner as the *dagga* with the exception that the load is centered. This drum is usually tuned to *Sa* for the singer, though in some cases it may be tuned to *Pa*.[85]

Hindusthani percussionists developed *bols* (a series of words which describe the pattern of strokes) for the playing and teaching of *tabla*. These serve the tablist in the same way that drum rudiments serve rudimental snare drummers. They provide a mnemonic aid which onomatopoetically describes the sound of the drum stroke. Like drum rudiments, the *bols* were used to teach rhythm patterns before they were placed in a written form. When the Hindusthani musicians did write them down, they continued to use the *bols*, merely notating them in letters. Unlike rudiments, the *bols* for *tabla* may be very complicated and do not conveniently translate to Western drum notation. It is important to maintain the differences of sound on the tabla. The simplest way to do this is for Western musicians to learn and adopt the Hindusthani written *bols*. As an aid to understanding the following *bols* for the *talas* listed, this key is provided for the various sounds. Common sounds include but are not limited to the following: *Dha, Dhin, Ge, Na, Thin, Ti, Ra, Ki, Ta, Kat, Tu, Tra* and *Ka*. The following pages include simple diagrams for the reproduction of these sounds on *tabla*. The following are only the basic patterns. Tablists are free to improvise and "make variations" upon them so long as the fundamental rhythm is not obscured.

Dha is usually used for the *sama* (strong beat) of the *tala*. It is made by playing both drums at once. The *dagga* (the larger, kettle-shaped drum on the left) is struck with the fingers of the hand while the palm pushes into the head modifying

---

[85]On evenings when several pitch centers are to be used the percussionist may choose to bring several *dyans*. Each *dyan* could be tuned to a specific pitch center before the evening's music begins. This saves a great deal of time in re-tuning the instruments.

the sound. The pitch rises and then falls as the pressure is released. The *dyan* (the smaller wooden drum on the right which is pitched to *Sa* or *Pa*) is played near the edge of the head and is allowed to ring.[86]

DHA
घ

Figure 3: *Dha*

Dhin is similar to *Dha*. The *Dagga* is played the same, but the *Dyan* is struck at the edge of the load. There is a noticeable change in both pitch and timbre. The drums are both still allowed to ring freely.[87]

DHIN
घीं

Figure 4: *Dhin*

Ge is the same stroke as *Dha* on the *Dagga*, but the *Dyan* is not struck.[88]

GE
गे

Figure 5: *Ge*

---

[86]Authors notes, "Notebook A," p. 46.

[87]Authors notes, "Notebook A," p. 46.

[88]Author's notes, "Notebook A," p. 47.

Na is similar to *Dha*. The *dyan* is struck as in *Dha*, but the *dagga* is not struck at all. This may be used for the *kali* (empty beat).[89]

NA
न

Figure 6: *Na*

Thin is similar to *Dhin*, but the *dagga* is not struck. The *dyan* is struck near the edge of the load with one finger.[90]

THIN
(teen)
तीं

Figure 7: *Thin*

The *bols* "*Ti, Ra, Ki* and *Ta*" are usually performed in that order as sixteenth notes. For *Ti* the *Dyan* is struck with the second third and fourth fingers of the right hand. The fingers land flat upon the head and stay there; there is no ring. For *Ra* the first finger of the right hand strikes the drum in the same way.[91]

TI
ती

RA
र

Figure 8: *Ti / Ra*

---

[89] Author's notes, "Notebook A," p. 46.

[90] Author's notes, "Notebook A," p. 46.

[91] Author's notes, "Notebook A," p. 46.

For *Ki*, the left hand is played flat against the drum head of the *dagga* with no ring. For *Ta* the first, second and third fingers of the right hand strike the *dyan* flat, again allowing no ring.[92]

Figure 9: *Ki* / *Ta*

Kat is made by striking the *dyan* with the four fingers of the right hand flat and solidly with no ring. *Kat* is often used for the *Kali*.[93]

Figure 10: *Kat*

Tu is similar to *Kat* except that the finger tips do not cover the load of the drum, but instead just reach it. There is a definite difference in pitch and in timbre. *Tu* may also serve as the *kali*.[94]

Figure 11: *Tu*

---

[92]Ibid.

[93]Author's notes, "Notebook A," p. 47.

[94]Author's notes, "Notebook A," p. 47.

Tra is a short "flam" made by striking the head of the *dyan* with the fourth, third and second fingers of the right hand in rapid succession. This is usually accomplished by striking the head with a glancing blow while moving the hand to the right. This is often followed by the *bol, Ka.*[95]

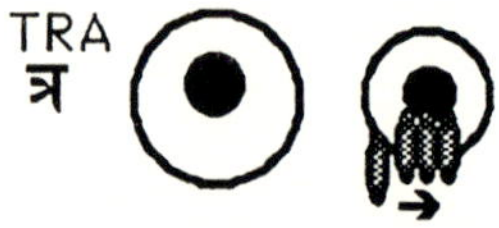

Figure 12: *Tra*

Ka is similar to *Ge*. The *dagga* is played with the tip of the finger at the edge of the load. For *Ka*, the palm is not pushed into the drum; there is no change of pitch or timbre. *Ka* is often associated with *Tra* following *Tra* by one eighth note.[96]

Figure 13: *Ka*

Talas used in *Bhajans*

Tala Bhajini has no specific *bols*. The percussionist(s) improvise(s) in 4/4 time with steady beats and little ornamentation (little of what is referred to by the phrase "make variation").[97]

---

[95] Author's notes, "Notebook A," p. 47.

[96] Author's notes, "Notebook A," p. 47.

[97] Author's notes, "Notebook B," p. 27.

Tala Teental has sixteen *matras* (counts). It is a very standard *tala* used for many *bhajans*. The *kali*[98] (empty beat) is on the ninth *matra*. The *bols* are arranged as follows:[99]

Dha Dhin Dhin Dha | Dha Dhin Dhin Dha |

Dha Thin Thin Ta | Ta Dhin Dhin Dha |

Example 29: *Tala Teental*

Tala Rupak has seven *matras* organized as 3+2+2. The *kali* is on the first *matra* (which may seem unusual to Western ears, since it is not an anacrusis, but the downbeat).[100]

Ti Ti Na | Dhi Na Dhi Na

Example 30: *Tala Rupak*

---

[98]The *kali* is represented here by the small circle "°" placed over the bol which is the *kali*.

[99]Author's notes, "Notebook B," p. 26.

[100]Author's notes, "Notebook B," p. 26.

Tala Dadra has six *matras* which are divided into two groups of three 3+3. It is very much like Western 6/8 time or even similar to waltz time. The *kali* is again on the first *matra*, though in this *tala* it may serve as an anacrucis.[101]

Dha Ge Na | Dha Ti Na

Example 31: *Tala Dadra*

Tala Kherva may be considered to have eight or four *matras*. The *kali* is on the fifth of the eight *matras*. The *bols* are as follows:[102]

Dha Ge Na Ti | Na Ka Dhin Na

Example 32: *Tala Kherva*

Other common *Talas* Usually Used in *Kirtan* or Solo Singing

---

[101] Author's notes, "Notebook B," p. 27.

[102] Author's notes, "Notebook B," p. 28.

Tala Ektal contains six *matras* arranged as 2+2+2 each of which is subdivided. The *kali* is found on the third *matra* (which may be considered the downbeat of the second measure in 2/4 time.[103]

Dhin-Dhin Dha-Tra-Ka | Tu-Na Kat-Ta | Dha-Tra-Ka Dhin-Nc

Example 33: *Tala Ektal*

Tala Vilambit Ektal, a very slow version of *Ektal*, adds further subdivisions. In it there are twelve *matras* arranged as follows the *kali* is on the seventh *matra* (the third beat of the second measure in 4/4 time).[104]

Dhin Dhin Dha-Ge Ti-Ra-Ki-Ta | Tu Na Kat Ta | Dha-Ge Ti-Ra-Ki-Ta Dhin Na

Example 34: *Tala Vilambit Ektal*

Tala Vilambit Tilvada is usually a very slow *tala*. It has sixteen *matras* arranged as below. The *kali* is on the ninth *matra* (the first beat of the third measure in 4/4 time.[105]

---

[103]Author's notes, "Notebook B," p. 27.

[104]Author's notes, "Notebook B," p. 29.

[105]Author's notes, "Notebook B," 31.

Dha Ti Ra Ki Ta Dhin --Dhin | Na Na Thin Thin |

Ta Ti Ra Ki Ta Dhin --Dhin | Na Na Dhin Dhin |

Example 35: *Tala Vilambit Tilvada*

Tala Jumra has fourteen *matras* arranged in two groups of seven 3+4 + 3+4. The *kali* is the only difference between the two groups. The *kali* is on the first beat of the third measure (the eighth *matra*). The mixed meter feeling is not very pronounced at slow tempos.[106]

Dhin --Dha Ti Ra Ki Ta | Dhin Dhin Dha Ge Ti Ra Ki Ta |

Thin --Ta Ti Ra Ki Ta | Dhin Dhin Dha Ge Ti Ra Ki Ta |

Example 36: *Tala Jumra*

Tala Tappa comes from the deserts of Rajasthan. It is said to represent the gait of the camel. Many happy songs are sung in this relatively slow *tala*. It contains sixteen *matras* arranged as 4+4+4+4 or 4/4 time. The *bols* are arranged as

---

[106]Author's notes, "Notebook B," p. 30.

below. Notice the off beat on every beat three and on the fourth beat of the third measure. The *kali* is on the ninth *matra* (beat one of the third measure).[107]

Example 37: *Tala Tappa*

Tala Deepchandi contains fourteen *matras* arranged as 3+4 + 3+4. Like *Tala Jumra*, the only difference between the two groups is the *kali* on the first beat of the second group. Because of the blank *matras* at the end of each measure, there is a definite feeling of mixed meter even in slower tempos.[108]

Example 38: *Tala Deepchandi*

---

[107]Author's notes, "Notebook B," p. 29.

[108]Author's notes, "Notebook B," p. 34.

62

Tala Dharmar contains an unusual combination of metric division. There
are fourteen *matras* divided as 5+2 + 3+4. The *kali* occurs on the eighth *matra* (the
downbeat of the third bar). The seventh and fourteenth *matras* are entirely blank,
which makes the next *matras* sound much stronger.[109]

Example 39: *Tala Dharmar*

[109]Author's notes, "Notebook B," p. 32.

CHAPTER 7
INDIGENIZED PRAYER

Bhajans and *kirtans* may be used in the rituals of the Catholic Church in every place where they are consistent with the requirements of the liturgy. Where the music called for by the liturgy is a song or hymn (the equivalent of *kirtan*), *kirtan* may be used. Where the liturgy calls for a litany, an antiphon, a simple responsory or a song, *bhajans* may be used. The *Ordo* (order of liturgies) includes two primary liturgies: The Liturgy of the Hours (LOTH) and the Mass. Each of the three Rites of the Church in India has its particular versions of these. In the interest of simplicity, the Latin Rite will be discussed here.

The Liturgy of the Hours

The Liturgy of the Hours is tied to the hours of the day and much can be said about the use of Hindusthani *ragas* for each hour of the day. It is important that the appropriate *raga* be used since this is an integral part of Hindusthani theory. There are today five "hours" within the Latin Liturgy of the Hours: The Office of Readings (Matins), Morning Prayer (Lauds), Daytime Prayer (a combination of Tierce, Sext, and Nones), Evening Prayer (Vespers) and Night Prayer (Compline). Each of these has a specific outline which is followed.[110]

The Office of Readings

The Office of Readings is most often celebrated before sunrise; however, it may be celebrated at any time of the day. It has the following order of worship:

Invitatory

---

[110]A. M. Roguet, O.P. *The Liturgy of the Hours: The General Instructions on the Liturgy of the Hours with a Commentary*, translated by Peter Coughlan and Peter Purdue (Collegeville, Minnesota: The Liturgical Press, 1971).pp. 28f.

Antiphon with Invitatory Psalm
Hymn (song)
Three psalms with antiphons
First Reading (Biblical) with responsory
Second Reading (patristic or hagiographical)
    with responsory
Te Deum (when used)
Prayer and dismissal[111]

The Invitatory versicle is a short dialogue between the presider and the assembly. The text is from the Ordinary. It might take the form of a *sloka* or short phrase sung to a two- or three-note tone. It might also take a simple *bhajan* form with the assembly answering the leader's phrase.

The Invitatory versicle is followed by the invitatory psalm (Psalm 95) with its appropriate antiphon. A psalm with antiphon is easily rendered in the litany form of *bhajan* and could be used by the assembly responding with the antiphon while the cantor sings the text of the psalm.

The hymn or song could easily be replaced by a *bhajan* or *kirtan* with a text suitable for the hour of the day in which the Office of Readings is celebrated. Seasonal texts which reflect the liturgical calendar are also useful at this point in the hours.

The psalmody, which is proper to the day, may be sung using the litany form of *bhajan* with the assembly singing the antiphon while the cantor or choir sings the verses of the psalm.

The readings are found in the proper for the day. The first reading is taken from the scriptures. It is followed by a responsory which closely resembles the *bhajan* form of direct repetition. The second reading is taken from writings of the early Church or from the lives of the saints. It is also followed by a responsory

[111]Roguet, pp. 32-4.

which may take the form of a direct repetition *bhajan*. These responsories would not be written-out compositions but freely improvised by the cantor.

The *Te Deum* is sung when called for and it could take the Indian form of *kirtan*.

The final prayer is proper to the day and may be chanted by the presider. The dismissal is a short dialogue and could take the Indian form of a *sloka*.

Morning Prayer

Morning Prayer should be celebrated early in the morning. It is a very important hour regarding music. The order of service is:

> Introductory verse
> Hymn (song)
> Psalmody
>> Morning Psalm
>> Canticle from the Hebrew Scriptures
>> Psalm of Praise
> Reading with responsory (song or spoken)
> Canticle of Zechariah with antiphon
> Prayers consecrating the day to God
> The Lord's Prayer
> Concluding prayer and dismissal[112]

Since Morning Prayer is always said in the early morning, the *ragas* used for morning prayer are those of dawn and morning. This includes the *ragas* from the following *thatts*: *Bilaval Thatt* including *Raga Bilaval*, *Raga Bhupali*, and *Raga Jansamohini* (See Example 3: *Bilaval Thatt*); *Bhairav Thatt* including *Raga Bhairav* and *Raga Jyogi* (See Example 10: *Bhairav Thatt*); *Bhairavi Thatt* including *Raga Bhairavi*, *Raga Mishra Bhairavi*, and *Raga Bilaskhani Todi* (See Example 23:

---

[112]Roguet, pp. 29-32.

Bhairavi Thatt); and *Todi Thatt* including *Raga Todi* (See above Example 27: *Todi Thatt*). These *ragas* belong to the break of day and to morning because of the notes (*swaras*) they contain (See Figure: 13: Time and *Raga*).

As in the Office of Readings, the introductory verse may be sung in the manner of an Indian *sloka*.

A *bhajan* or *kirtan* may be substituted for the morning hymn. This song usually praises God for his gift of the new day, though its text may also reflect the season or the feast of the day.

The psalmody may be sung in the form of a litany *bhajan* with the assembly taking only the antiphon. The psalm prayers may be chanted by the presider in the manner of a *sloka*.

The reading, which is proper to the day, is followed by a responsory. It may take the form of a direct repetition *bhajan*.

The Canticle of Zechariah may either take the form of a litany *bhajan* with the assembly singing the antiphon, or the form of *kirtan* with everyone singing together.

It is possible to sing the prayers which consecrate the day to God, but this is seldom done. The Indian bishops encourage the assembly to formulate their own prayers for particular needs at this point.

The Lord's prayer may be spoken or sung together as a *kirtan*.

The concluding prayer is taken from the proper and may be chanted by the presider.

The dismissal, if sung, may take the form of a *sloka*

Daytime Prayer

Daytime prayer is a combination of the three minor hours. It is often said instead of sung and has little importance musically. It occurs in the middle of the day. The Order of service is:

> Introductory verse
> Hymn (song)
> Psalmody (three psalms)
> Reading with responsory
> Prayer and dismissal[113]

As with the other hours, the introductory verse may be sung. It is followed by a hymn suitable for the mid-day which may be a *bhajan* or a *kirtan*. Since this hour may be celebrated anytime between 10: A.M. and 3:00 P.M., the appropriate *ragas* for the hour should be used.

The psalmody, which is proper to the day, may take the form of a litany *bhajan* with the assembly singing the antiphon.

The reading is followed by a responsory which may take the form of a direct repetition *bhajan*.

The concluding prayer, which is proper to the day, and dismissal may be chanted as in the other hours.

Evening Prayer

Evening Prayer should be celebrated at dusk when daylight fades. It also is a very important hour regarding music. The order of service is:

---

[113]Roguet, pp. 35-6.

> Introductory verse
> Hymn (song)
> Psalmody
>> Evening or incense Psalm
>> Psalm of Praise
>> Canticle from the Christian Scriptures
> Reading with responsory (song or spoken)
> Canticle of Mary with antiphon
> Prayers of petition
> The Lord's Prayer
> Concluding prayer and dismissal[114]

Since evening prayer occurs at dusk, it is appropriate that the *ragas* of sunset be used. These include the *ragas* from the following *thatts*: *Khamaj Thatt* including *Raga Khamaj*, and *Raga Kalawati* (See Example 7: *Khamaj Thatt*); *Poorvi Thatt* including *Raga Poorvi* (See Example 13: *Poorvi Thatt*); *Marva Thatt* including *Raga Marva* (See Example 15: *Marva Thatt*). These choices are made on the basis of the relationship of particular notes of the *raga* to the hour of the day (See Figure 13: Time and *Raga*). If the music is for later in the hour *Asavari Thatt* may be used. These include *Raga Asavari*, *Raga Malkauns* and *Raga Dharbari Kanada*. These *ragas* are used after sundown.

The introductory verse of Evening Prayer may be sung using one of the above *ragas* with the assembly making its appropriate responses.

The introductory verse is followed by an evening hymn. There is an ancient Eastern tradition to light the evening lamp at this point. A *bhajan* proclaiming Christ as the light of the world may be used here. A *kirtan* may also be substituted which deals with the light of Christ or the season of the liturgical year.

The psalmody is proper to the day. It often includes the incense psalm (Psalm 141 "Let my prayer come like incense before you; the lifting up of my hands

---

[114]Roguet, pp. 29-32.

like the evening sacrifice."[115]). A *bhajan* of incense in the litany form may be used here. The other psalm and canticle from the Christian Scriptures may be sung in the manner of a litany *bhajan* also with the assembly singing only the antiphon.

The proper reading is again followed by a responsory which may take the form of a direct repetition *bhajan*.

The Canticle of Mary may follow the form of a litany *bhajan* or the form of a *kirtan* with all the assembly singing. The following example was written in English for the celebration of 100 years in India of the Salesian Missionaries of Mary Immaculate.

Magnificat

Music: Dr. Fr. Charles Vas, S.V.D., D. Mus.
Text: Melville Mendonca
Raga: Asavari

My soul does mag- ni- fy the Lord. My spi- rit re-
joi- ces in God my Sa- viour. My soul does mag- ni- fy the Lord.
1) I sing of the love of my God. I call Him my
king and re- deem- er. He knows all my weak- ness for-
gives all my sins. I praise the name of the Lord.

2.   He shows me His might and His power.
      The proud He will strip of their grandeur.

---

[115]Confraternity of Christian Doctrine, *New American Bible,* (New York: Catholic Book Publishing Company, 1970), Psalm 141: 2.

70

The humble He draws to the throne of His love.
I praise the Name of the Lord.

3.   The joys I recall in my life
Have come from my God and my saviour.
He sees in my heart all the efforts to change.
I praise the Name of the Lord.

4.   Give thanks to the Lord, O my soul,
Give thanks and give praise for His mercy,
His mercy to all who abide by His Word.
O praise the Name of the Lord.[116]

The prayers of petition may be sung, but are usually spoken by the people of the assembly each asking for a particular intention.

The Lord's prayer may be sung as a *kirtan*.

The proper concluding prayer may be chanted with the dismissal taking the form of a *sloka*.

Night Prayer

Night prayer is the final prayer at the end of day before going to bed. The Order of service is:

Introductory verse (with examination of conscience)

Hymn (song)

Psalmody

Reading with responsory

Canticle of Simeon

Prayer and dismissal

Marian antiphon (seasonal)[117]

---

[116]Copyright © 1989 Fr. Dr. Charles Vas, SVD, D.Mus. Used with permission. All rights reserved.

[117]Roguet, pp. 36-7.

Night Prayer occurs after sundown; the *ragas* belonging to the night are appropriate for use with it. These *thatts* include: *Kalyan Thatt* including *Raga Kalyan* (See Example 1: *Kalyan Thatt*); *Kafi Thatt* including *Raga Kafi* (see Example 17 *Kafi Thatt*).

Though this hour is often prayed by the individual it may be prayed by a community in choir. The introductory verse may be chanted by the presider with the assembly making its response in an appropriate *raga*.

The introduction is followed by an examination of conscience; this may include the use of the *Kyrie* (which may then be sung as a direct repetition *bhajan*) or a *bhajan* petitioning God for his mercy.

The hymn may be a *bhajan* or a *kirtan* appropriate to the hour.

The proper psalm may again be sung as a litany *bhajan*.

The proper reading is followed again by a responsory which may take the form of a direct repetition *bhajan*.

The Canticle of Simeon may be sung by the assembly in the form of *kirtan* or as a litany *bhajan* with the assembly singing the antiphon alone.

The prayer and dismissal may be chanted as before using appropriate *ragas*.

The five *Marian Antiphons* whose texts vary with the seasons of the liturgical year may be replaced with Marian *bhajans* with similar texts. The N.B.C.L.C. provides an entire tape devoted to *Marian Bhajans*.

The Mass

The liturgy of the Mass is central to the Catholic faith. It is the source and summit of the worship life of the Church. All three Rites have their own versions

72

of this liturgy. The following order of service and musical discussion is taken from the Latin Rite, though the same substitutions are possible in the corresponding places of the Syro-Malabar and Syro-Malankara Rites.

INTRODUCTORY RITES

Before the Mass begins the assembly may gather and sing *bhajans* as a sign of community and unity in Christ.

Entrance Song

The entrance song may be a *bhajan* or *kirtan* with appropriate words. The antiphon for the introit may be sung as a direct repetition *bhajan*.

Adaptation(s) for India:
The people may leave their shoes outside the chapel.
The people may leave offerings near the entrance to the chapel.
During the entrance Rites, bhajans may be sung while the priest is welcomed by the assembly with a single arati. The Priest then welcomes the assembly with the same arati.
On solemn occasions a candle stand with five or seven candles [or oil lamps] may be used.
The priest venerates the altar by touching it with his hands and then bringing his hands to his eyes.
When incense is used, it can be placed in the Indian censer with a handle.[118]

Greeting

Adaptation for India:

---

[118]International Committee on English In the Liturgy, Inc., *Roman Missal* Special Masses and adaptations for India by the C.B.C.I. Commission for Liturgy (Bangalore, India: Brothers and Fathers of the Society of St. Paul, 1986), p. 357.

The priest and the assembly may remain standing throughout the liturgy or may squat on the floor in traditional Indian posture through the entire celebration or during the entrance and the Liturgy of the Word.[119]

Penitential Rite (Either Sprinkling Rite or Penitential Rite)

Sprinkling Rite

The *Asperges Me* (Cleanse me, O Lord) may be sung in the manner of a *kirtan* or it may be replaced by a *bhajan* with suitable text. A five-fold purification rite is possible here as had been approved by the C.B.C.I.

Penitential Rite

The Lord Have Mercy (Kyrie) may be sung in the manner of a direct repetition *bhajan*, or it may be replaced by a *bhajan* with appropriate text.

Adaptation(s) for India:
The penitential rite may conclude with the *pachanga pranam* (placing the hands feet and head in contact with the floor). While in this posture, the presiding minister speaks the words of absolution. Then they sit back and exchange a sign of peace and reconciliation such as the *anjala hasti* (bowing to one another with hands joined on the chest) or by placing the hands of the giver between those of the receiver in Syro-Malabar fashion.[120]

Glory to God in the highest (Gloria, seasonal use):

---

[119]*Roman Missal* (India), p. 357.

[120]*Roman Missal* (India), p. 367.

The Glory to God may be sung in the manner of an Indian *kirtan* using the appropriate *raga* for the time of day.

LITURGY OF THE WORD

First reading   (Spoken)

Responsorial Psalm

The psalm may be sung in the manner of a litany *bhajan* with the people singing only the antiphon while the cantor or choir sings the text of the palm.

Second Reading   (Spoken)

Gospel Acclamation

The gospel acclamation may be sung in the manner of a direct repetition *bhajan* or an appropriate *bhajan* or *sloka* may be substituted.

Gospel   (Spoken)

Homily   (Spoken)

Profession of Faith (Creed)

The creed is seldom sung, but it would be possible to sing it in the manner of a *kirtan.*

General Intercessions

The General Intercessions may be sung, but in India the bishops encourage the faithful to speak their own petitions which makes singing problematic.

Adaptation for India:

As in Indian custom intentions may be formulated and spoken spontaneously by the people. The universal aspect of the Church and her prayer is not to be forgotten.[121]

LITURGY OF THE EUCHARIST

Preparation of the Gifts and the Altar

The song for the preparation of the Gifts and the altar may be a *bhajan* or *kirtan* suitable for this point in the liturgy.

Adaptation for India:
The corporal may be replaced by a suitable metal tray.

Adaptation for India:
At the offertory a tray with eight flowers may be included for *pushpa arati*.

As each of the flowers is placed about the tray, an invocation based upon one of the attributes of Jesus is said or sung:

Om shri Yeshu bhagavate namah	Jesus, the Lord
Om shri deva putrâya namah	Jesus, the Son of God
Om shri mariya putrâya namah	Jesus the Son of Mary
Om Shri deva narâya namah	Jesus, the God-man
Om Shri sat purushâya namah	Jesus, the true person
Om shri Yeshu abhishiktaya namah	Jesus, the anointed
Om shri sad guruve namah	Jesus, the true teacher
Om shri taraneshâya namah	Jesus, the Saviour.[122]

Eucharistic Prayer (*anaphora*)

---

[121]*Roman Missal* (India), p. 372.

[122]*N.B.C.L.C. Bhajans*, p. 87.

Holy, Holy, Holy
The Mystery of Faith (Acclamation)
Great Amen.

Each of the eucharistic acclamations may be sung in the manner of an Indian *kirtan* with the use of *ragas* appropriate to the time of day.

Adaptation for India:
At the words "through him ..." the celebrant lifts the tray upon which are placed the chalice and paten while triple *arati* is done by designated members of the assembly. *Pushpa arati* (with flowers), *dhupa arati* (with incense), and *deep arati* (with flame) are added to the ringing of the bell.[123]

Adaptation for India:
The ministers and the assembly may then make their reverence through the use of the *anjali hasta* (as a profound bow with the hands joined at the forehead), a *pachanga pranam* (touching the head, hands and feet to the ground), or as a *sushtanga pranam* (full prostration). [124]

COMMUNION RITE

The Lord's Prayer

The Lord's prayer may be chanted in the manner of an Indian *kirtan* using a *raga* appropriate to the hour of the day.

Sign of Peace
Breaking of the Bread

---

[123]*Roman Missal* (India), p. 469.

[124]*Roman Missal* (India), p. 469.

The acclamation for the Breaking of the Bread (*Agnus Dei*) may be sung in the manner of a direct repetition *bhajan*, a litany *bhajan* or an Indian *kirtan*. The *raga* used should be appropriate to the hour of the day.

Communion

The Communion Song may be a *bhajan* or *kirtan* with words appropriate for communion. The *raga* should reflect the time of day of the celebration.

A period of silence or song of praise follows communion. *Bhajans* (particularly *namajapa*) and *kirtan* are useful in bringing the assembly to a quiet contemplation of God. Such contemplation is highly recommended by the N.B.C.L.C. The *ragas* used should be appropriate for the hour of the day.

Prayer after Communion

This prayer is taken from the proper. It may be sung in the manner of an Indian *sloka*. The *raga* used should reflect the time of day and the assembly should answer with a sung amen.

CONCLUDING RITE

> Greeting
> Blessing
> Dismissal

These may be sung in the manner of an Indian *sloka* with the assembly singing their appropriate parts. Again, the *ragas* used should reflect the time of day.

The Mass ends at the dismissal. Liturgists are free to plan music here in any form. In India, the use of *namajapa*, or *bhajan* is highly suggested at this point to bring the assembly into the quiet contemplation of the God who dwells within each person.

Nonliturgical Functions

In the same way that *bhajans* and *kirtan* may be used throughout the public liturgies of the church, they may also be used in devotional practices. Where song is allowed (and encouraged) in devotions, these forms may be used. It is also possible to have entire services of *bhajan* singing as well as services where well known *kirtan* are chanted by the assembly. The creativity of those who prepare services will in large be the determining factor of how these forms are used.

One form of Indian prayer called *dyanna* is worth particular mention. In this form the devotee(s) begin with a *mantra* (short prayer invocation). They begin speaking or singing it and gradually are reduced to silence with the prayer finally resting on the breath in and out of the devotee. This is a form of centering prayer. *Bhajans* and *namajapa* are particularly useful for groups wishing to experience this prayer together.

CHAPTER 8
CONCLUSIONS

The fathers of the Second Vatican Council challenged the clergy throughout the world to make the liturgy more accessible, more meaningful to the assembly. Inculturation especially with music and language has gone a long way toward accomplishing that goal. In India the use of *bhajans* and *kirtan* have provided a much needed cultural link with the indigenous people. However, there are a number of problems in dealing with indigenized liturgy in such a large and diverse country as India.

All of India does not share a Hindu cultural background. The tribal peoples (animists) who have converted to Christianity find the imposition of Hindu culture upon their worship to be as foreign as the Latinizations of the Portuguese. The Catholic Bishops' Conference of India realizes this and is working towards regional centers of liturgy which find inculturation into the local tribal life to be their goal. About this Fr. Jacob Theckanath (N.B.C.L.C. staff) stated:

> In the Centre [N.B.C.L.C.] here we do not have all the data about it [work with tribal inculturations] but people have been doing a lot [in their regions]. ... but not much literature is available. It is done in the tribal dialect [not in one of the national languages]. ... They have their own type of music and dance, which they use for celebration. ... For this we need to have an office to promote this music and to support them. ... [To] provide them with experts in music; these are the services which should be done. ... We need to have much more ... but for this we are understaffed. But even if we don't have [the] staff here, there is a way of working. [We can] bring these experts here for consultation and preparation.[125]

Language is also a great problem for the Church in India. There are so many languages used throughout the country that no central office can begin to deal with them adequately. Linguist/liturgists are needed for every region of the country to oversee the adaptation of the services to that region in appropriate ways. Father

---

[125]Reverend Jacob Theckanath, interview by author, Tape recording, Bangalore, India, 12 September, 1990.

Jacob remarked, "As a National Centre we have a problem with languages." He went on to comment on the multiplicity of languages and cultures throughout the country and that in all areas "We [the N.B.C.L.C.] need to compose in the vernacular" both in language and in musical style. He commented that the bishops were supportive of efforts to provide texts and music in all the various languages of the country.

> We have been able to get that kind of support [from the bishops] for
> the variety of languages and cultural differences that we promote
> here in our celebrations and training programs. We have people of
> all backgrounds and we make them express in worship and song in
> their own way. For instance we have Mass in three Rites here, all
> three Rites as a regular feature for every seminar. ... So that gives
> everyone the opportunity to enter into the spirit of the other Rites.[126]

It is also noted that there are forces which would prefer to return to the music of the past, particularly in the well-established Syro-Malabar parishes. This tug of war in seemingly opposite directions is unnecessary. The documents of the Council clearly allow the use of both. Music which has served the Church in India for more than a thousand years (Syrian chant) does not need to be replaced by *bhajan* and *kirtan*. Rather, such chant is augmented by the use of the indigenized forms in worship. Fr. Jacob commented on this by saying that "We have the ... group who doesn't want any changes as well as the group that wants all changes. So that problem is there."

The differences in the foundation of the three Rites causes some problems. In the Southern State of Kerela where the Thomas Christians have lived for almost two thousand years, the desire to maintain their tradition is both strong and legitimate. In the North where Christianity arrived with the Portuguese, the people seem more open to the adaptations of Indian music and culture for the liturgies.

> In the parishes, I have heard in my visits to the North *bhajan* singing
> for the Eucharistic celebrations and the people do like them. ... In
> another fifteen/twenty years, I feel if you were to come back you
> would see a different type of singing [all indigenous] at the

---

[126]Reverend Jacob Theckanath, interview by author, Tape recording, Bangalore, India, 12 September, 1990.

Eucharist, especially in the North Indian Dioceses. In the South it may take a longer time. Pockets of Christianity: Bangalore, Goa, Mangalor [all Portuguese foundations], Kerela [Thomas Christians] -- you will find resistance to it. [Because when they were originally converted they were forced to renounce all Hindu culture.] Everything Hindu was [considered] diabolical. ... A lot of [Hindu] customs had been incorporated into their [Thomas Christians] lifestyle. ... Then came the Latinization of the Syro Malabar.[127]

Another problem area is the difference between the culture of a modern metropolitan area and that of village India. On the whole, the people in village India seem more ready to accept the use of indigenized prayer than do the people of the cities.

[In the villages] they have no problem, you can sing *bhajans* all night. They will be there with you. It is only in the sophisticated cities that we have a problem. ... They think that being Indian is not worth [anything; it is pagan].[128]

About the place of the N.B.C.L.C. in exploring and teaching inculturations to the Church in India Fr. Jacob stated:

The bishops consider us to be rendering a unique service to the Church. They know we are a little bit avant garde, but they know they can trust [us]. ... Our loyalty is to Christ, to the Church ... to the spirit of the Council [Vatican II] ... I am basically very hopeful, optimistic ... We have done quite a bit in the last twenty-five years. For us [the Church in India] it is a gigantic task.[129]

The leaders of the Catholic Church in India are optimistic about the future. Despite all its problems the Church continues to grow and prosper. The

---

[127]For example the *thali* (the tieing of a small golden ornament about the neck of the bride) was replaced with the Western wedding ring. The wedding ring was a non-Christian custom adapted for use by the Church in the West. The *thali* was forbidden for many years by the Latinization of the Thomas Christians. Reverend Jacob Theckanath, interview by author, Tape recording, Bangalore, India, 12 September, 1990.

[128]Reverend Jacob Theckanath, interview by author, Tape recording, Bangalore, India, 12 September, 1990.

[129]Reverend Jacob Theckanath, interview by author, Tape recording, Bangalore, India, 12 September, 1990.

inculturations which have been accepted by the people seem to truly help foster a spirit of prayerfullness and openness to the will of God.

> As regards the celebration of the Eucharist in the Indian way that we are having here at the Centre, that will spread across the country much more in the coming years. ... We need to make it much more suited to the different regions of India. ... What happens here is the celebration is influenced by Sanskrit tradition and [the] Sanskrit language, which is obviously not suitable for people in the different areas of India. ... There is need for adaptation in the regions not by us [N.B.C.L.C.]. The various regional groups [of bishops] have to do that.
>
> We [at the N.B.C.L.C.] need to do more by way of animation of liturgical music in the country, as a national organization. We have had one seminar for music animators -- one training program. This interaction and orientation has to continue. Perhaps we have to do more, we in this [N.B.C.L.C.] community. We may have to plan more, to bring the music animators/composers [here], and continue to increase the momentum of inculturation.
>
> ... If we have more people coming to do inculturation of music, and depending on how much we push, we give -- we can! I am hopeful. That is what I want to say, I am hopeful. ... On the whole when you look at the [entire] country, I am very positive. After all, it is only twenty five years since the Council is over...[130]

The future of inculturation in India seems bright. The uses of *bhajan* and *kirtan* in the liturgies of the Church are assured. It is left to the creativity of liturgical musicians in all the regions of India to create compositions in these forms suitable for use in the liturgy.

---

[130]Reverend Jacob Theckanath, interview by author, Tape recording, Bangalore, India, 12 September, 1990.

SOURCES CONSULTED

PUBLISHED MATERIALS

All-India Liturgical Meeting (V). *Statement of the V All-India Liturgical Meeting.* Bangalore, India: N.B.C.L.C., 1976.
All-India Liturgical Meeting (VI). *The Unfulfilled Quest.* Bangalore, India: N.B.C.L.C., 1983.
All-India Liturgical Meeting (VII). *Ministers For a Pastoral Liturgy.* Bangalore, India: N.B.C.L.C., 1986.
All-India Liturgical Meeting (VIII). *Listening and Worshipping Community.* Bangalore, India: N.B.C.L.C., 1988.
_____ *Report and Statement of the VIII All-India Liturgical Meeting.* Bangalore, India: N.B.C.L.C., 1988.
Amaladoss, M., S. J. "*Bhajan* As Prayer." N.B.C.L.C. Seminar Leaflet Series no. 9. Bangalore, India: N.B.C.L.C.
_____ "Indigenous Theology and Spirituality." Bangalore, India: N.B.C.L.C.
_____ "Liturgical Renewal and Ecclesiastical Law." N.B.C.L.C. Seminar Booklet Series no. 35. Bangalore, India: N.B.C.L.C.
_____ "*Namajapa.*" N.B.C.L.C. Seminar Leaflet Series no. 10. Bangalore, India: N.B.C.L.C.
Amaldos, Swami. *Yeshu Abba Consciousness.* Bangalore, India: Asian Trading Corporation, 1986.
Amalorpavadass, Father D. S. "Basic Structure of Liturgical Action." N.B.C.L.C. Seminar Leaflet Series no. 6. Bangalore, India: N.B.C.L.C.
_____ "Gospel and Culture." N.B.C.L.C. Mission Theology for Our Times no. 11. Bangalore, India: N.B.C.L.C., 1978.
_____ "Inculturation Is Not Hinduisation." N.B.C.L.C. Inculturation Series no. 6. Bangalore, India: N.B.C.L.C., 1985.
_____ "Inculturation." N.B.C.L.C. Inculturation Series no. 8. Bangalore, India: N.B.C.L.C.
_____ "Inculturation Realizes the Church's Universality, Fullness and Unity." N.B.C.L.C. Inculturation Series no. 7. Bangalore, India: N.B.C.L.C.
_____ "Indian Culture." N.B.C.L.C. Inculturation Pamphlet Series no. 16. Bangalore, India: N.B.C.L.C., 1980.
_____ "Liturgy Relevant to Life." N.B.C.L.C. Seminar Booklet Series no. 4. Bangalore, India: N.B.C.L.C., 1978.
_____ *Milieu of God-Experience.* Bangalore, India: National Biblical Catechetical and Liturgical Centre, 1982.
_____ "Relation Between the Gospel and Culture." N.B.C.L.C. Inculturation Series no. 4. Bangalore, India: N.B.C.L.C.
_____ "Theological Basis of an Authentic Inculturation." N.B.C.L.C. Inculturation Pamphlet Series no. 5. Bangalore, India: N.B.C.L.C.
_____ "Towards Indigenization in the Liturgy." N.B.C.L.C. Theology for Our Times no. 6. Bangalore, India: N.B.C.L.C.
Amalorpavadass, Father D. S. "Towards Indigenization in the Liturgy." N.B.C.L.C. Seminar Leaflet Series no. 7. Bangalore, India: N.B.C.L.C., 1975.

84

Amalorpavadass, Father D. S., ed. *Indian Christian Spirituality*. Bangalore, India: N.B.C.L.C., 1982.
_____. *Post Vatican Liturgical Renewal In India (1963-1968)*. Bangalore, India: N.B.C.L.C., 1968.
_____. *Post Vatican Liturgical Renewal In India vol. II (1968-1972)*. Bangalore, India: N.B.C.L.C., 1972.
_____. *Post Vatican Liturgical Renewal In India (1971-1974)*. Bangalore, India: N.B.C.L.C., 1976.
_____. *Post Vatican Liturgical Renewal In India (1974-1976)*. Bangalore, India: N.B.C.L.C., 1977.
_____. "Statements on Non-Biblical Scriptures." Bangalore, India: N.B.C.L.C., 1976.
Analytical Greek Lexicon. London: Samuel Bagster and Sons Limited, 1975.
Anand, Father Subhash, Th.D. "*Amrtamanthana*: Life Beyond Life." *The Adyar Library Bulletin*, 1989: Offprint.
_____. "A Beast In Search of Humanity: The Elephant God." *Vidyajyoti Journal of Theological Reflection*. July 1988: Offprint.
_____. "The Light-Bearing Dark Night." *Vidyajyoti Journal of Theological Reflection* vol. LIV no. 2. (February 1990): Offprint.
_____. "A Mass For a Liberated People." Pune, India: By the author, Papal Seminary J.D.V. 1988.
_____. *Savitri* and *Satyavat*. Annals of the Bhandakar Oriental Research Institute. vol. LXIX 1988: Offprint.
An Intermediate Greek-English Lexicon: Founded Upon the Seventh Edition of Liddell and Scott's Greek-English Lexicon. Oxford, England: Clarendon Press, 1983.
Attwater, Donald. *Churches in Communion With Rome. The Christian Churches of the East*, Revised ed. Milwaukee, Wisconsin: The Bruce Publishing Company, 1961.
_____. *Churches Not In Communion With Rome. The Christian Churches of the East*, Revised ed. Milwaukee, Wisconsin: The Bruce Publishing Company, 1962.
Bandoypadhayaya, Shripada. *The Music of India*. Bombay, India: D. B. Taraporevala Sons and Company Private Limited, 1970.
Barnstone, Willis, ed. *The Other Bible: Jewish Pseudepigrapha, Christian Apocrypha, Gnostic Scriptures, Kabbalah, Dead Sea Scrolls*. San Francisco: Harper Collins Publishers, 1984.
Bartholomew World Travel Map. *Indian Subcontinent: India, Pakistan, Bangladesh, Sri Lanka*. Edinburgh, Scotland: John Bartholomew and Sons, Limited. 1987.
_____. *Middle East*. Edinburgh, Scotland: John Bartholomew and Sons, Ltd. 1991.
Bishops' Committee on the Liturgy. *Music in Catholic Worship*. Washington D. C.: United States Catholic Conference, 1972.
Bishops' Committee on the Liturgy. *Liturgical Music Today*. Washington D. C.: United States Catholic Conference, 1982.
Boff, Father Leonardo, O.F.M. *God's Witnesses in the Heart of the World: Testigos de Dios en el Corazón del Mundo*. Translated and Edited by Robert Fath. Chicago: Claret Center for Resources in Spirituality, 1981.
Booch, Harish S. *One and Unique Pocket Guide to Bombay: A Visitor's Companion*. Bombay, India: Lakhani Book Depot, 1990.

Bor, Joep. "The Voice of the Sarangi." *Quarterly Journal of the National Centre for the Performing Arts.* Vol. XV and XVI nos. 1,3, and 4 combined reprint, Bombay: National Centre for the Performing Arts, 1987.

Catholic Bishops' Conference of India. "Celebration of the Eucharist in Indigenous Form." *Saccidananda* Series no. 1. Bangalore, India: N.B.C.L.C. Cassette with 86 slides.

_____Commentary on Adaptations in the Liturgy. N.B.C.L.C. Seminar Booklet Series no. 47. Bangalore, India: N.B.C.L.C., 1981.

_____*Conclusions of the Seminar for Composers of Liturgical Music.* Bangalore, India: N.B.C.L.C., 1980.

_____*Indian Art and Architecture.* Color slides [illustrating "Milieu of God-Experience."] Bangalore, India: N.B.C.L.C., 1982.

_____Music sub-Committee. "Music for the Ministerial Parts of the Mass." Bangalore, India: C.B.C.I. Commission for Liturgy, 1970.

_____*N.B.C.L.C. Bhajans: A Collection of Songs of Praise in Various Languages Used At the N.B.C.L.C.* Bangalore, India: N.B.C.L.C., 1988.

_____*N.B.C.L.C. Bhajans: Music Edition in Staff Notation.* Bangalore, India: N.B.C.L.C., 1977.

_____*An Order of the Mass for India.* Bangalore, India: N.B.C.L.C., 1984.

_____*Roman Missal.* Bangalore, India: Brothers and Fathers of the Society of Saint Paul, 1986.

_____*Sharing Worship* (January 20-25, 1988). Bangalore, India: N.B.C.L.C., 1989.

_____"Statement of Facts On the First Stages of Liturgical Indigenization." Bangalore, India: N.B.C.L.C.

_____*Texts for the Masses for Four Saints Specially Connected With India.* Bangalore, India: N.B.C.L.C., 1981.

Catholic University of America. *New Catholic Encyclopedia.* New York: McGraw-Hill Book Company, 1967.

Chidbhavananda, Swami. *Facets of Brahman.* Tiruchiapalli (Trichy), India: Sri Ramakrishna Tapovanam, 1985.

Choudhary, J.D., MA, JI., comp. *Concise Hindi-English Dictionary.* New Delhi, India: Kiran Publications.

Colunga, Rev Alberto, O.P. and Rev. Laurentio Turrado. *Biblia Sacra iuxta Vulgatam Clementinam*, Nova Editio. Matriti: Biblioteca De Autores Cristianos, 1965.

Confraternity of Christian Doctrine. *New American Bible.* New York: Catholic Book Publishing Company, 1970.

Daniélou, Alain [Shiva Sharan]. *Northern Indian Music.* Calcutta:Visva Bharati, 1949.

_____Northern Indian Music, revised. New York: Frederick A. Praeger, 1968.

Day, C. R. *The Music and Musical Instruments of Southern India and the Decan.* Delhi, India: B. R. Publishing Company: 1981; Reprint 1983.

De Mello, Father Anthony, S.J. *Sadhana, A Way to God: Christian Exercises in Eastern Form.* Garden City, New York: Doubleday and Company, 1984.

Deshpande, Vamanrao H. *Indian Musical Traditions: An Æsthetic Study of the Gharanas in Hindustani Music.* Translated by S. H. Deshpande. Bombay, India: Popular Prakasham, 1973.

Desroches, Father John, C.S.C. and George Joseph *India Today*. Bangalore, India: Centre For Social Action, 1988.

Deva, B. Chaintanya. *Indian Music*. New Delhi, India: Indian Council for Cultural Relations, 1974.

Divry, George C., general editor. *Divry's Modern English-Greek and Greek-English Dictionary*. New York: D.C. Divry, Inc. Pub. 1971.

Egan, Harvey D., S.J. *Christian Mysticism: the Future of a Tradition*. New York: Pueblo Publishing Company, 1984.

Emhardt, William Chauncy, K.S.S., K.S.H.S. and George M. Lamsa. *The Oldest Christian People: A Brief Account of the History and Traditions of the Assyrian People and the Fateful History of the Nestorian Church*. With a forward by Rt. Reverend John Gardiner Murray, Presiding Bishop of the Protestant Episcopal Church of America [1926]. New York: A.M.S. Press, 1970 reprint, New York 1926.

Encyclopædio [sic] *of Indian Music* With Special Reference to the *Ragas*. New Delhi, India: Sri Satguru Publications, 1988.

Flannery, Father Austin, O.P., ed. *Vatican Council II: The Conciliar and Post Conciliar Documents*. Collegeville: The Liturgical Press, 1975.

Fortescue, Adrian Ph.D., D.D. *The Lesser Eastern Churches*. New York: A.M.S. Press, 1972; reprint, London: Catholic Truth Society, 1913.

Fox-Strangeways, Arthur H. *The Music of Hindostan*. Oxford: Clarendon Press, 1967.

French, R. M., translator. *The Way of a Pilgrim*. New York: Ballantine Books, 1974.

Gautam, M. R. *The Musical Heritage of India*. New Delhi, India: Abhinav Publications, 1980.

Gispert-Sauch, Father George, S.J. "An Informal Sharing on *Om*." Inculturation Pamphlet Series no.2. Bangalore, India: N.B.C.L.C.

Government Survey of India. *Road Map of India*. Delhi, India: Makhija Brothers, 1988.

Grant, Michael. *Ancient History Atlas 1700BC to AD565*. London: Weidenfeld and Nicolson, 1976.

Griffiths, Bede. "*Om* As the Word of God." Inculturation Pamphlet Series no.1. Bangalore, India: N.B.C.L.C.

Harper Atlas of World History. New York: Harper and Row, 1987.

Hesselgrave, David J. *Communicating Christ Cross-Culturally*. Bangalore, India: St. Paul Publications, 1978.

Holroyde, Peggy. *Indian Music: A Vast Ocean of Promise*. With a forward by Pandit Ravi Shankar. London: George Allen and Unwin Limited, 1972.

Hutchinson, Gloria. *Six Ways to Pray From Six Great Saints*. Cincinnati, Ohio: St. Anthony Messenger Press, 1982.

Imber, Walter and Hans Boesch, editors. *India*. New Delhi: Oxford and IBH Publishing Co., 1975.

Indian Liturgical Association. *Celebrants All: Liturgical Formation in Seminaries and Formation Houses*. Bangalore, India: Indian Liturgical Association, 1990.

"In Memoriam: D.S. Amalorpavadass" *Bishop's Committee on the Liturgy Newsletter* XXVI (October/November 1990), 44. Washington D.C.: National Conference of Catholic Bishops

International Committee on English in the Liturgy. *The Rites of the Roman Catholic Church: As Revised by Decree of the Second Vatican Ecumenical*

Council and Published by Authority of Pope Paul VI. Volumes I, II, and IA. New York: Pueblo Publishing Company, 1976.

_____*The Roman Missal.* Bangalore, India: The Brothers and Fathers of the Society of St. Paul, 1973.

_____*The Sacramentary.* New York: Catholic Book Publishing Company, 1985.

Iyer, T.G.S. Balaram. *History and Description of Sri Meenakshi Temple.* Madurai, India: Sri Karthik Agency, 1988.

Jairazbhoy, N.A. *The Rags* [sic] *of North Indian Music.* London: Faber and Faber, 1971.

Jones, E. Stanley. *The Christ of the Indian Road.* New York: The Abingdon Press, 1925.

Kaufmann, Walter. *The Ragas of North India.* Bloomington, Indiana: Indiana University Press, 1968.

Keifer, Ralph, ed. *To Give Thanks and Praise.* Washington D.C.: The Pastoral Press, 1980.

Keifer, Ralph, ed. *To Hear and Proclaim.* Washington D.C.: The Pastoral Press 1983.

Keskar, B.V. *Indian Music Problems and Prospects.* Bombay: Popular Prakashan, 1967.

Keating, Abbot Thomas,O.S.C.O., M. Basil Pennington, O.S.C.O., and Thomas E. Clarke, S.J. *Finding Grace At the Center.* Still River, Massachusetts: St. Bede Publications, 1977

Khayyath, E. *Syri Orientales Seu Chaldæi Nestoriani et Romanorum Pontificum Primatus.* Rome 1870.

Kolencherry, Antony. *Universality of Modern Hinduism.* Bangalore, India: Asian Trading Corporation, 1984.

Krishnaswami, S. *Musical Instruments of India* revised. New Delhi, India: Publications Division, Ministry of Information and Broadcasting Government of India, 1965 revised 1971.

Kykkotis, I., *English Greek and Greek English Dictionary.* London: Lund Humphries and Co. Ltd., 1947.

Luc, Sr. Therese. 100 Years Salesian Missionaries of Mary Immaculate. Bangalore, India: St. Paul Press Training School, 1989.

Malieckal, Father Louis, C.M.I. *Yajna and Eucharist.* Bangalore, India: Dharmarum Publications, 1989.

Martin, R. Montgomery, ed. *The Illustrated Atlas and Modern History of the World.* London: John Tallis and Company, 1851. Reprinted and edited as: *Antique Maps of the 19th Century World.* Hong Kong: Portland House, 1989.

Mascaró, Juan, translator. *The Bhagavad Gita.* Harmondsworth, Middlesex, England: Penguin Books Limited, 1962.

May, Herbert G., ed. *Oxford Bible Atlas.* 3rd ed. New York: Oxford University Press, 1990.

McBrien Father Richard. *Catholicism.* San Francisco: Harper and Row, Publishers, 1981.

McKinnon, Frederick R., ed. *Thirty Years of Liturgical Renewal: Statements of the Bishops' Committee on the Liturgy.* Washington, D.C.: United States Catholic Conference, 1987.

Menen, Raghava R. *The Sound of Indian Music.* New Delhi, India: Indian Book Company, 1976.

Merton, Thomas. *The Last of the Fathers: Saint Bernard of Clairvaux and the Encyclical Letter* Doctor Mellifluus. New York: Harcourt Brace Jovanovich, Publishers, 1954.

Mookenthotlam, Father Anthony ,M.S.F.S. *Towards a Theology in the Indian Context.* Bangalore, India: Asian Trading Corporation, 1980.

Narasimhan, Chakravarthi V. *The Mahabharata: An English Version Based on Selected Verses.* New York: Columbia University Press, 1965.

Neil, Rev. John Mason, M.A. *A History of the Holy Eastern Church.* New York: A.M.S. Press, 1976; reprint, London: Joseph Masters, 1850.

Neil, Most Rev. Stephen. *The Story of the Christian Church in India and Pakistan.* Grand Rapids, Michigan: William B. Eerdmans Publishing Company, 1970.

Pakkirisamy, K.V. *Tanjore and Big Temple.* Thanjavur (Tanjore), India: Vetrivel Press, 1955.

Panikkar, Raimundo. *The Unknown Christ of Hinduism.* Bangalore, India: Asian Trading Corporation, 1981.

_____. *The Vedic Experience, Mantramañjarî.* Pondicherry, India: All India Books, 1977.

Pathak, Prof. R. C., ed. *Bhargava's Standard Illustrated Dictionary of the Hindi Language (Hindi-English Edition) Revised and Enlarged.* Varanasi, India: Bhargava Bhushan Press, 1971.

Pathikulangara, Varghese. *Chaldeo-Indian Liturgy.* Rome: Oriental Institute of Religious Studies, 1982.

_____. *Church and Celebration.* Kottayam, India: Denha Services, 1986.

Popidara, Father Placid, C.M.I. *The Canonical Sources of the Syro-Malabar Church.* Rome: Oriental Institute of Religious Studies, 1986.

Pothan, S. G. *The Syrian Christians of Kerala.* Bombay, India: Asia Publishing House, 1963.

Prabhupada, A.C. Bhaktivedanta Swami. *Bhagavad-Gita As It Is,* abridged ed., New York: Bhaktivedanta Book Trust, 1976.

Prajnanananda, Swami. *A History of Indian Music: (Ancient Period)* vol. 1. Calcutta: Ramakrishna Vedanta Math, 1963.

Puthanangady, Father Paul, S.D.B., ed. *Liturgy for Christian Living.* Bangalore, India: N.B.C.L.C., 1987.

_____. *Report of the Sixth All India Liturgical Meeting* (November 29 - December 3, 1983). Bangalore, India: N.B.C.L.C., 1984.

_____. *Report of the Seventh All India Liturgical Meeting* (December 10-15, 1986). Bangalore, India: N.B.C.L.C., 1989.

_____. *Report of the Eighth All India Liturgical Meeting* (December 4-8, 1988). Bangalore, India: N.B.C.L.C., 1990.

_____. *Sharing Worship.* Bangalore, India: N.B.C.L.C., 1988.

Radhakrishnan, Sarvepalli and Charles A. Moore, editors. *A Sourcebook in Indian Philosophy.* Princeton: Princeton University Press, 1957.

Rajan, Father Jesu. *Bede Griffiths and Sannyasa.* Bangalore, India: Asian Trading Corporation, 1989.

Roguet, A.M. *The Liturgy of the Hours: The General Instructions on the Liturgy of the Hours with a Commentary.* Translated by Peter Coughlan and Peter Purdue. Collegeville, Minnesota: The Liturgical Press, 1971.

Saldanha, Father Julian, S.J. *Inculturation.* Bangalore, India: St. Paul Publications, 1987.

Sambamurthy, P. *South Indian Music, Vol. I-V.* Madras, India: The Indian Music Publishing House, 1983.

Sen, Kshiti Mohan. *Hinduism.* London: Penguin Books Limited, 1961. Reprint 1987.

Shirali, Vishnudass. *Sargam: An Introduction to Indian Music.* New Delhi: Abhinav/ Marg Publications, 1977.

Taft, Father Robert, S.J. *The Liturgy of the Hours in the Christian East.* Kerela, India: K.C.M. Press, 1983.

T.T. Maps. *Guidebook to India's Railways.* Madras, India: T.T. Maps and Publications Private, Limited, 1988.

Uma Publications. *Bangalore, Mysore, Ooty: A Tourist Guide Book With City Maps Completely Revised and Updated.* Bangalore, India: Vasan Book Depot, 1989.

Vadakkel, Father Jacob. *The East Syrian Anaphora of Mar Theodore of Mopsuestia.* Rome: Oriental Institute of Religious Studies, 1989.

Van Leeuwen, Father Gerwin, O.F.M., ed. *Searching for an Indian Ecclesiology.* Bangalore, India: Asian Trading Corporation, 1984.

Vas, Father Charles, S.V.D., Dmus. *Madhur Geet.* Bombay, India: Sangeet Abhinay Academy, 1989.

Veer, Ram Arta. *The Music of India.* New Delhi, India: Pankaj Publications, 1986.

Vidal-Naquet, Pierre, ed. *The Harper Atlas of World History.* Cambridge, Massachusetts: Harper and Row Publishers, 1986.

Walker, Benjamin. The Hindu World: An Encyclopedic Survey of Hinduism. New York: Frederick A. Praeger, Publishers, 1968.

Walker, Williston revised by Cyril C. Richardson, Wilhelm Pauck and Robert Handy. *A History of the Christian Church.* revised ed. New York: Charles Scribner's Sons, 1959.

Watson, Francis. *A Concise History of India.* New York: Thames and Hudson, Inc., 1974.

Zimmer, Heinrich. *Philosophies of India*, Bollingen Series XXVI. Edited by Joseph Cambell. Princeton: Princeton University Press, 1951.

INTERVIEWS

Arokiosamy, Father. A., C.S.C. and Sr. Marie Jacinta, MA. Interview by author.
Tape recording. N.B.C.L.C. Bangalore, Karnataka, India. June 20, 1990.

Eucharistic celebration, Father Jacob Theckanath, presiding celebrant. Tape
Recording by author. N.B.C.L.C. Bangalore, Karnataka, India. June 20, 1990.

Eucharistic celebration, Father Paul Puthanangady, S.D.B. presiding celebrant.
Tape Recording by author. N.B.C.L.C. Bangalore, Karnataka, India. June 22, 1990.

Eucharistic celebration, Syro-Malabar (Malayalam) Tape recording by author.
Dharmarum Chapel, Bangalore, Karnataka, India. June 26, 1990.

Cheruvil, Father Alexander, C.S.C. Interview by author. Tape recording. Holy
Cross Provincial House, Bangalore, Karnataka, India. June 23, 1990.

Edappily, Father John, C.M.I., MTh, MA, MA, ThD. Interview by author.
Dharmarum College, Bangalore, Karnataka, India. June 26, 1990.

Student recital. Tape recording by author. Dharmarum College, Bangalore,
Karnataka, India. June 26, 1990.

Eucharistic celebration with Benediction (Tamil). Tape recording by author. St.
Mary's Basilica, Bangalore, Karnataka, India. June 30, 1990.

Eucharistic celebration (English) Tape recording by author. Resurrection Parish,
Bangalore, Karnataka, India. July 1, 1990. Eucharistic celebration, Syro-
Malabar (Malayalam) Tape recording by author. Dharmarum Chapel, Bangalore,
Karnataka, India. July 3, 1990.

Eucharistic celebration (English). Tape recording by author. Holy Cross
Seminary, Pune, Maharashtra, India. July 9, 1990. D'Silva, Father Harry,
C.S.C. Interview by author. Tape recording. Holy Cross Seminary,
Pune, Maharashtra, India. July 9, 1990.

Eucharistic celebration (English). Tape recording by author. Holy Cross
Seminary, Pune, Maharashtra, India. July 13, 1990.

Eucharistic celebration (English). Tape recording by author. Holy Cross
Seminary, Pune, Maharashtra, India. July 14, 1990.

Vas, Father Charles, S.V.D., Dmus. Interview by author. Tape recording.
Sangeet Abhinay Academy, Bandra, Maharashtra, India. July 18, 1990.

_____. Interview by author. Tape recording. Sangeet Abhinay Academy,
Bandra, Maharashtra, India. July 23, 1990.

_____. Interview by author. Tape recording. Sangeet Abhinay Academy,
Bandra, Maharashtra, India. July 24, 1990.

_____. Interview by author. Tape recording. Sangeet Abhinay Academy,
Bandra, Maharashtra, India. July 25, 1990.

_____. Interview by author. Tape recording. Sangeet Abhinay Academy,
Bandra, Maharashtra, India. July 26, 1990.

_____. Interview by author. Tape recording. Sangeet Abhinay Academy,
Bandra, Maharashtra, India. July 27, 1990.

_____. Interview by author. Tape recording. Sangeet Abhinay Academy,
Bandra, Maharashtra, India. July 28, 1990.

_____. Interview by author. Tape recording. Sangeet Abhinay Academy,
Bandra, Maharashtra, India. July 29, 1990.

_____. Interview by author. Tape recording. Sangeet Abhinay Academy,
Bandra, Maharashtra, India. July 30, 1990.

_____. Interview by author. Tape recording. Sangeet Abhinay Academy, Bandra, Maharashtra, India. July 31, 1990.

_____. Interview by author. Tape recording. Sangeet Abhinay Academy, Bandra, Maharashtra, India. Tape 2, July 31, 1990.

_____. Interview by author. Tape recording. Sangeet Abhinay Academy, Bandra, Maharashtra, India. August 1, 1990.

_____. Interview by author. Tape recording. Sangeet Abhinay Academy, Bandra, Maharashtra, India. August 2, 1990.

_____. Interview by author. Tape recording. Sangeet Abhinay Academy, Bandra, Maharashtra, India. August 3, 1990.

_____. Interview by author. Tape recording. Sangeet Abhinay Academy, Bandra, Maharashtra, India. August 8, 1990.

_____. Interview by author. Tape recording. Sangeet Abhinay Academy, Bandra, Maharashtra, India. August 9, 1990.

Eucharistic celebration (Tamil). Tape recording by author. Infant Jesus Shrine, Bangalore, Karnataka, India. August 16, 1990.

Tour of Anjali Ashram. Tape recording by author. Anjali Ashram, Mysore, Karnataka, India. August 28, 1990.

Liturgical prayers. Tape recording by author. Anjali Ashram, Mysore, Karnataka, India. August 28, 29, 1990.

Sister Jacinta. Interview by author. Tape recording. N.B.C.L.C., Bangalore, Karnataka, India. September 8, 1990.

Sister Jacinta. Interview by author. Tape recording. N.B.C.L.C., Bangalore, Karnataka, India. September 10, 1990.

Theckanath, Father Jacob. Interview by author. Tape recording. N.B.C.L.C., Bangalore, Karnataka, India. September 12, 1990.

DISCOGRAPHY

Allarakha, Ustad and Zakir Hussain. *Together*. Cassette. Fort, Bombay, India: Magnasound (India) Private, Limited, 1990.

Anand, Father Subhash, ThD. *Premdhara Vol. I*. Cassette. Pune, India: By the author, unreleased.

_____ *Premdhara Vol. II*. Cassette. Pune, India: By the author, unreleased.

_____ *Premdhara Vol. III*. Cassette. Pune, India: By the author, unreleased.

_____ *Premdhara Vol. IV*. Cassette. Pune, India: By the author, unreleased.

_____ *Premdhara Vol. V*. Cassette. Pune, India: By the author, unreleased.

Bhuriya, Father Mahipal. *Premanjali: Hindi* Pune, India: XIC Studios.

_____ *Premanjali: Instrumental*. Pune, India: XIC Studios.

Bhuriya, Father Mahipal. Xpd'n [*Spandan 1: Moods & Movements.*] Pune, India: By the author, available through *Ishvani Kendra*.

Chaurasia, Pandit Hari Prasad. *Pandit Hari Prasad Charasia Vol.I*. Cassette. New Delhi, India: Super Cassette Industries Limited, 1990.

_____ *Pandit Hari Prasad Charasia Vol.II*. Cassette. New Delhi, India: Super Cassette Industries Limited, 1990.

Christuraj, M., S.V.D. *Ishvani Bhajans Vol I*. Pune, India: *Ishvani Kendra*.

_____ *Ishvani Bhajans Vol II*. Pune, India: *Ishvani Kendra*.

_____ *Ishvani Bhajans Vol III*. Pune, India: *Ishvani Kendra*.

Dey, Aloke Nath. *Dusk to Dawn: Musical Mosaic of Melodic Variations on Sarod, Sarangee, Santoor, Sitar, Violin, Guitar, and Flute*. Cassette. Calcutta, India: The Gramophone Company of India Limited, 1987.

Ghosh, Dhruba. *Soulful Sarangi*. Cassette. Fort, Bombay, India: Magnasound (India)Private, Limited, 1989.

Giriraj, Pandit. *Evocative Music on Sitar*. Cassette. Fort, Bombay, India: Magnasound (India) Private, Limited, 1989.

Hussain, Ustad Ali Ahmad. *Ustad Ali Ahmad Hussain: Shehnai*. Cassette. Calcutta, India: The Gramophone Company of India Limited, 1987.

Ishvani Kendra. *Bhajanjali*. Pune, India: Ishvani Kendra.

_____ *Varthayin Virundhu Vol. I*. Cassette. Pune India: Ishwani [sic] Communications.

_____ *Varthayin Virundhu Vol. II*. Cassette. Pune India: Ishwani [sic] Communications.

Jalota, Anup. *Meera Bhajans: All Traditional Bhajans*. Cassette. Bombay, India: Music India Limited, 1987.

Janaki, S. *Meera Bhajans: Hindi*. Cassette. Madras, India: The Master Recording Company, 1986.

James, Father, M.L., C.M.I. and A. V. Thomas Johnson. *Sandesh: Christian Songs*. Sagar, India: *Jyoti Bhavan*, 1989.

James, Father, M.L., C.M.I. and Father Anto Amarnad, C.M.I. *Upasana: Christian Bhajans*. Sagar, India: *Jyoti*, 1988.

John Paul, Father, S.V.D. and Father Norbert Herman, S.V.D. *Geet Aur Ghazal*. Cassette. Pune, India: *Ishvani Kendra*.

*Kalai Kaviri. Anmavin ragangal Kalai Kaviri*Tiruchiappali, Tamil Nadu, India.

_____ *Deiveega Sandhangal* Tiruchiappali, Tamil Nadu, India.

_____ *Agama Jyoti Kalai Kaviri*Tiruchiappali, Tamil Nadu, India.

Khan, Ustad Bismillah. *Shehnai Recital*. Cassette. Calcutta, India: The Gramophone Company of India Limited, 1989.

Khan, Ustad Usman and Father M. Christuraj, S.V.D. *Deep Calls to Deep.*
Cassette. Pune, India: Ishvani Communications.
_____*Ishvani Instrumental Vol II.* Pune, India: Ishvani Communications.
Kochappilly, Father Paulachan, C.M.I. and Father Paul Poovathingal, C.M.I.
Aradhana: Christian Bhajans. Sagar, India: Jyoti Bhavan, 1989.
Louise, Sister, S.R.A. *Madhur Vani Bhajans.* Cassette. Bandra, India. Sangeet
Abhinay Academy.
Mangeshkar, Lata. *Bhajans From Films.* Cassette. Calcutta, India: The
Gramophone Company of India Limited, 1982.
_____*Ram Ratan Dhan Payo.* Cassette. Bombay, India: Music India Limited,
1983.
Mangeshkar, Lata and Anup Jalota. *Bhajanmala.* Cassette. Bombay, India: Music
India Limited, 1984.
Mangeshkar, Lata and Hridaynath Mangeshkar. *Meera Bhajans.* Cassette.
Calcutta, India: The Gramophone Company of India Limited, 1980.
National Biblical, Catechetical and Liturgical Centre. *N.B.C.L.C. Bhajans Vol IA.*
Bangalore, India: N.B.C.L.C.
_____*N.B.C.L.C. Marian Bhajans.* Bangalore, India: N.B.C.L.C.
_____*N.B.C.L.C. Bhajans Vol IA.* Bangalore, India: N.B.C.L.C.
_____*N.B.C.L.C. Bhajans Vol IB.* Bangalore, India: N.B.C.L.C.
_____*N.B.C.L.C. Bhajans Vol IIA.* Bangalore, India: N.B.C.L.C.
_____*N.B.C.L.C. Bhajans Vol IIB.* Bangalore, India: N.B.C.L.C.
_____*N.B.C.L.C. Bhajans Vol III.* Bangalore, India: N.B.C.L.C.
Palackal, Joseph, Father Anto Amarand, Father James Muttickal and Sister Edith
F.M.M., *Christian Bhajans and Hymns.* Cassette. Bangalore, India:
Deccan Records Private Limited, 1987.
Parameswara, Annamanada. *Pancha Vadyam: Kerala Folk Instru   mental Music.*
Cassette. Calcutta, India: The Gramophone Company of India Limited,
1972.
Rakha, Ustad Alla, Arjun Shejwal, Pandit Shanta Prasad, Ustad Zakir Hussain,
and Jnan Prakash Ghosh. *Rhythm on Indian Drums.* Calcutta, India: The
Gramophone Company of India Limited, 1989.
Rao, Vijay Raghav. *Authentic Flute Music of India.* Cassette. Century City,
California: Olympic Records.
Shankar, Pandit Ravi. *The Spirit of Freedom Concerts.* Cassette. Bombay, India:
C.B.S. Gramophone Records and Tapes (India) Limited, 1990.
Sharma, Pandit Shivkumar. *Pandit Shivkumar Sharma In Concert Vol I.* Cassette.
Calcutta, India: The Gramophone Company of India, Limited, 1987.
_____*Pandit Shivkumar Sharma In Concert Vol II.* Cassette. Calcutta, India:
The Gramophone Company of India, Limited, 1987.
Sheila, Sister, C.M.C. *Santinadam.* Cassette. Trichur, India: Mercy College,
Palghat, 1989.
_____*Udayageetam: Christian Bhajans.* Cassette. Trichur, India: C.M.C.
Benefactors Trust, 1990.
Vas, Father Charles, S.V.D., Dmus. *Christian Devotional Songs (Malayalam)
Vol. I* Cassette. Bandra, India: Sangeet Abhinay Academy.
_____*Christian Devotional Songs (Malayalam) Vol. II* Cassette. Bandra,
India: Sangeet Abhinay Academy.
_____*Konkani Bhajans.* Cassette. Bandra, India: Sangeet Abhinay Academy.
_____*Madhur Geet Bhajans Vol. I* Cassette. Bandra, India: Sangeet Abhinay
Academy.

_____*Madhur Geet Bhajans Vol. II* Cassette. Bandra, India: Sangeet Abhinay Academy.

_____*Madhur Geet Hymns Vol. I.* Cassette. Bandra, India: Sangeet Abhinay Academy.

_____*Madhur Geet Hymns Vol. II.* Cassette. Bandra, India: Sangeet Abhinay Academy.

_____*Madhur Geet Hymns Vol. III.* Cassette. Bandra, India: Sangeet Abhinay Academy.

_____*Madhur Geet Hymns Vol. IV.* Cassette. Bandra, India: Sangeet Abhinay Academy.

_____*Madhur Sangeet Vol. I.* Cassette. Bandra, India: Sangeet Abhinay Academy.

_____*Madhur Sangeet Vol. II.* Cassette. Bandra, India: Sangeet Abhinay Academy.

_____"*Nabulo, Nabulo, Mere Pita* (Agony Song)." Cassette. Bandra, India: Sangeet Abhinay Academy, unreleased.

APPENDIX A

OFFICIAL DOCUMENT OF THE HOLY SEE
APPROVING THE 12 POINTS OF ADAPTATION
CONCILIUM AD EXEQUENDAM CONSTITUTIONEM
DE SACRA LITURGIA[131]

(true copy)   Vatican City, April 25, 1969

Prot. N. 802/69

To: Most Rev. D. Simon Lourdosamy
Archbishop's House
18, Miller's Road
Bangalore - 6, India

Your Excellency,

The Cardinal President of the "Consilium", His Eminence Benno Cardinal Gut, has accepted the proposals of the Catholic Bishops' Conference of India for certain adaptations in the liturgy, according to articles 37-40 of the Liturgical Constitution. In his name I would like to establish what follows:

1. The posture during Mass, both for the priests and the faithful, may be adapted to local usage, that is, sitting on the floor, standing and the like; footwear may be removed also.

2. Genuflections may be replaced by the profound bow with the anjali hasta.

3. A panchanga pranam by both priests and faithful can take place before the liturgy of the Word, as part of the Penitential rite, and at the conclusion of the Anaphora.

4. Kissing of objects may be adapted to local custom, that is, touching the object with one's fingers or palm of one's hand and bringing the hands to one's eyes or forehead.

5. The kiss of peace could be given by the exchange of the anjali hasta and/or the placing of the hands of the giver between the hands of the recipient.

6. Incense could be made use of more in liturgical services. The receptacle could be the simple incense bowl with handle.

7. The vestments could be simplified. A single tunic-type chasuble with a stole (angavastra) could replace the traditional vestments of the Roman rite. Samples of this change are to be forwarded to the "Consilium".

8. The corporal could be replaced by a tray (thali or thamboola thattu) of fitting material.

9. Oil lamps could be used instead of candles.

10. The preparatory rite of the Mass may include:
    a) the presentation of gifts

---

[131]Catholic Bishops' Conference of India, "A Commentary on Adaptations in the Liturgy." Seminar Booklet Series no. 47. Bangalore, India: N.B.C.L.C. pp.7-8.

b) the welcome of the celebrant in an Indian way, e.g. with a single
   arati, washing of hands, etc.
c) the lighting of the lamp
d) the greeting of peace among the faithful in sign of
   mutual reconciliation.

11. In the "Oratio fidelium" some spontaneity may be permitted both with regard to its structure and the formulation of the intentions. The universal aspect of the Church however should not be left in oblivion.

12. In the Offertory rite, and at the conclusion of the Anaphora the Indian form of worship may be integrated, that is, double or triple "arati" of flowers, and/or incense, and/or light.

The above mentioned adaptations can be put into effect by the Episcopal Conference and local hierarchies in places where they see fit and in the degree and measure that they think fitting for the faithful. A catechesis, however, should precede such changes, and if necessary, a gradual implementation could be done.

The proposal to compose a new Indian Anaphora in collaboration with experts in different fields is most welcome. When completed, copies should be sent to the "Consilium" for study. It might help if this were not publicized too much.

With hope and prayers that these adaptations will help the people of India, so noted for their spiritual inclination, to deepen their lives in the Paschal Mystery, I am

Respectfully yours in Christ,

(Sd)   A. Bugnini, C.M.,
Secretary.

APPENDIX B

LETTER FROM THE CHALDEAN BISHOP (UNIATE)
OF THE EPARCHY OF ST. THOMAS THE APOSTLE
CHALDEAN CATHOLIC DIOCESE - U.S.A.

Eparchy of St. Thomas the Apostle
Chaldean Catholic Diocese in the U.S.A.
25585 Berg Road
Southfield, Michigan 48034 U.S.A.
Telephone (313) 356-0565; 356-0569

April 25, 1991

Mr. Stephen F. Duncan
Coordinator of Liturgical Music
13235 Jefferson Ave.
P. O. Box 41679
Memphis, TN 38174-1679

Dear Mr. Duncan:

I have received your letter of April 17, 1991 regarding some questions about the
history of the Chaldean Church or Church of the East, here is the answer:

First of all the Syro Malabar Rite is a Chaldean Rite, it was under the jurisdiction of
the Patriarch of the East, Patriarch of the Seleucia - Ctesiphon till 1599 when the
Synod of Diamper decided to break with the Chaldean Church in Mesopotamia and
to be directly under the jurisdiction of the Pope in Rome.
The Syro Malankara are under the jurisdiction of the Syrian Orthodox Patriarch of
Antioch (Jacobites).
However, there is another branch of the Syro-Malabar who are till now under the
jurisdiction of the Nestorian Patriarch - Church of the East:

The actual situation is as follows:

        The Chaldean Patriarchate or the Patriarch of Babylon, with the See in
Baghdad, Iraq, which my diocese is part of it. Our actual Patriarch is Mar Raphael
I Bidawid.

        The Nestorian Church, or the Church of the East: non-Catholic branch, its
Patriarch is in Chicago, U.S.A. Mar Denha, IV.
Both Patriarchs claim to be the successors of St. Thomas, one Catholic and another
non-Catholic.

        There is another Nestorian Patriarch with residence in Baghdad. His
community was separated from the Nestorian church because the late Patriarch Mar
Shimun XXIII decided to follow the Gregorian calendar, a portion of this

Patriarchate was separated, and a patriarch was ordained to head this portion in keeping the same name church of the East, Nestorian church.

I hope these information are helpful to you.

With all best wishes, I am

Sincerely yours in Christ,

(Signed)
Most Reverend Ibrahim N. Ibrahim
Bishop of St. Thomas the Apostle,

Chaldean Diocese - U.S.A.

APPENDIX C

A BRIEF HISTORY OF CATHOLICISM IN INDIA

The development of music on the subcontinent of India (See Figure 14 - Political Map of India, 1991) is inextricably bound to the history of the peoples who have inhabited India. This includes the political, cultural, socioeconomic, philosophic, and religious components which influenced the development of the Catholic Church, as well as the development of Indian classical music. The birth and growth of Hinduism in its various forms began with the Dravidians in the South and the Aryans in the North. The Greek influence upon India occurred both through trade and conquest. There are religious and political influences from Persia which included the sending of Christian Bishops from the Seleucian Patriarch. Islam left its mark in the secular music of the North. European colonialism and the development of the Latin Rite Church in India were responsible for drastic changes in the Christian Church on the subcontinent. All of these influences on music are reflected in that used for the Rites of the Catholic Church in India today.

Dravidian India (before the Coming of the Aryans)

The Western name for India is derived from the area surrounding the river Indus (*Sindhu*) which flows through what is today Northwestern India and Pakistan. Set apart from the Asian continent by the Himalayan Mountain range on the North and East and the Mountains of Hindu Kush on the Northwest, the subcontinent of India was in effect isolated from the rest of the world (see Figure 15 - Land Features of the Subcontinent). Southern India with its seaports may have been more in touch with the rest of the world than were the villages in the north-central plains and the Punjab. Although trade through the high passes in the Himalayas was possible, it was easier to trade with the lands bordered by the Arabian Sea and the Indian Ocean. (See Figure 3 - Water Commerce.)[132]

---

[132]Watson, p. 11.

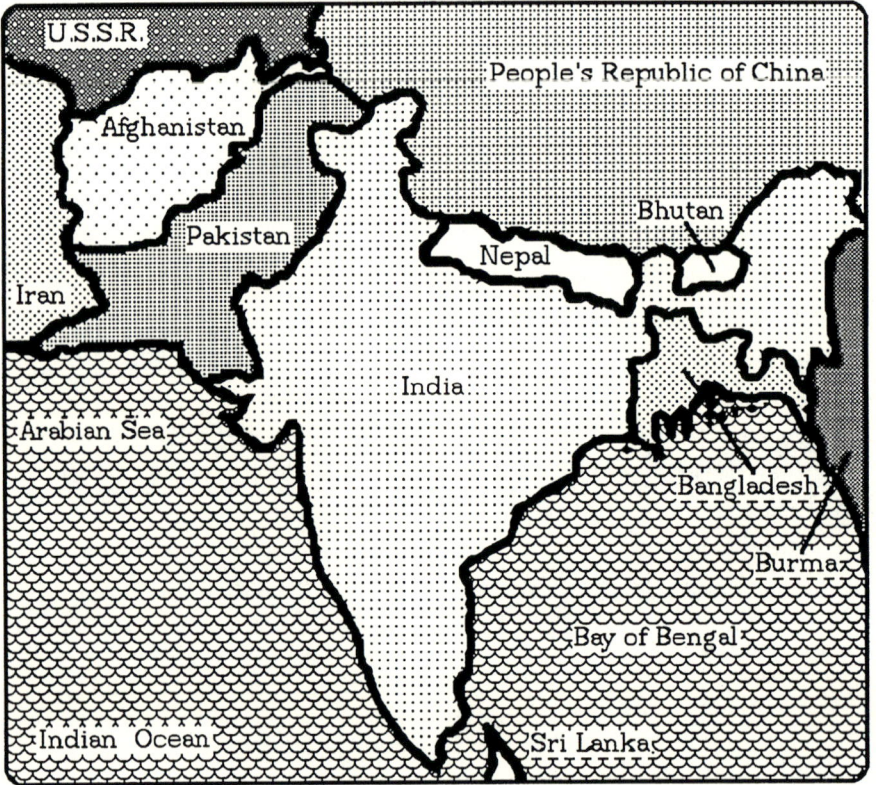

Figure 14
Political Map of India, 1991.[133]

---

[133]Adaptation from the *Bartholomew World Travel Map -- Indian Subcontinent.*

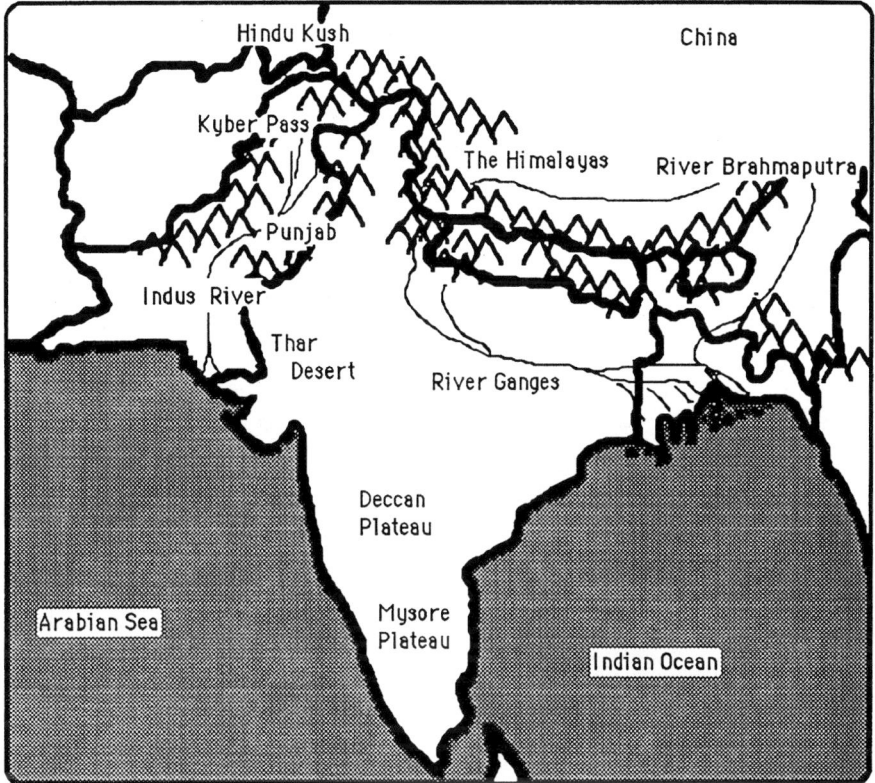

Figure 15
Land Features of the Subcontinent[134]

The earliest cultures found in India were loosely associated tribes, each with its own culture and religious beliefs. Tribes lived and flourished throughout the rich subcontinent. Little is known of these earliest inhabitants of India though it is presumed that the religious beliefs were totemic and animist. The descendants of

---

[134]"The World," Supplement to the *National Geographic*, December 1981, p. 780 A, Vol. 160, No. 6. *Bartholomew World Travel Map -- Indian Subcontinent: India, Pakistan, Bangladesh, Sri Lanka.* (Edinburg Scotland: John Bartholomew and Sons, Limited, 1987)

some of these tribes still exist today in some places in India (often as what is called a scheduled tribe).[135]

The Dravidian culture is considered to be one of the most important of the indigenous Indian cultures by many historians and archaeologists. The Dravidian culture was in existence through much of India before the coming of the Aryans. Hinduism in its Dravidian forms begins with the early Dravidian Indians. Unfortunately, there exist no known written records of the period. The great Aryan immigration is believed to have occurred between 2,000 BCE and 1500 BCE There is arguably some connection between the culture of the Dravidians and the culture of Babylon and Syria during these early years which continues to the present day[136]. Most probably this was a contact made through ocean-borne trade and travel rather than through land-based trade.

The difficult mountain passes through the Hindu Kush, the great impassable expanse of the Himalayas and the Great Indian Desert (*Thar* Desert) made land transportation prohibitively expensive. The Malabar coast of Southwestern India as well as the Coromandel Coast of Southeastern India show a great deal of contact from water-borne transportation. (See Figure 16.) The *ghatts* or mountains which divide Tamil Nadu from Kerela made travel there difficult, while ships could easily pass south of Cape Comorin.[137] The Dravidian culture continues to be predominant in the South of India today. The modern Indian States of Tamil Nadu, Kerela and Karnataka all have cultural ties will the ancient Dravidians. These Dravidians spoke a version of the *Tamil* language which is the state language of Tamil Nadu. The Dravidian peoples had begun to develop their ideas about religion and philosophy.

---

[135]Watson, pp. 21f.

[136]It may be well to point out that the Thomas Christians of India accepted both priests and bishops sent to them from the patriarch of Babylon (Chaldean Rite). The Christians of Syria and Babylon also have a traditional affiliation to the apostle Thomas since he is also held as the founder of the Christian Church in Babylon. Letter to author from the Most Reverend Ibhrahim N. Ibrahim, Bishop of the Eparchy of St. Thomas the Apostle, Chaldean Diocese, U.S.A.

[137]The name for the language of Kerala is "Malayalam," which means "from the mountains to the sea," a fitting name for the language of the inhabitants of a state which extends the length of the coast from the mountains to the sea.

As mentioned before these religious and philosophical systems were influenced by other ancient Near-Eastern cultures. Dravidian Hinduism was born during this time and would flourish throughout the land. Each town and village had its *avatar* or incarnation of god, in effect its patron saint.[138]

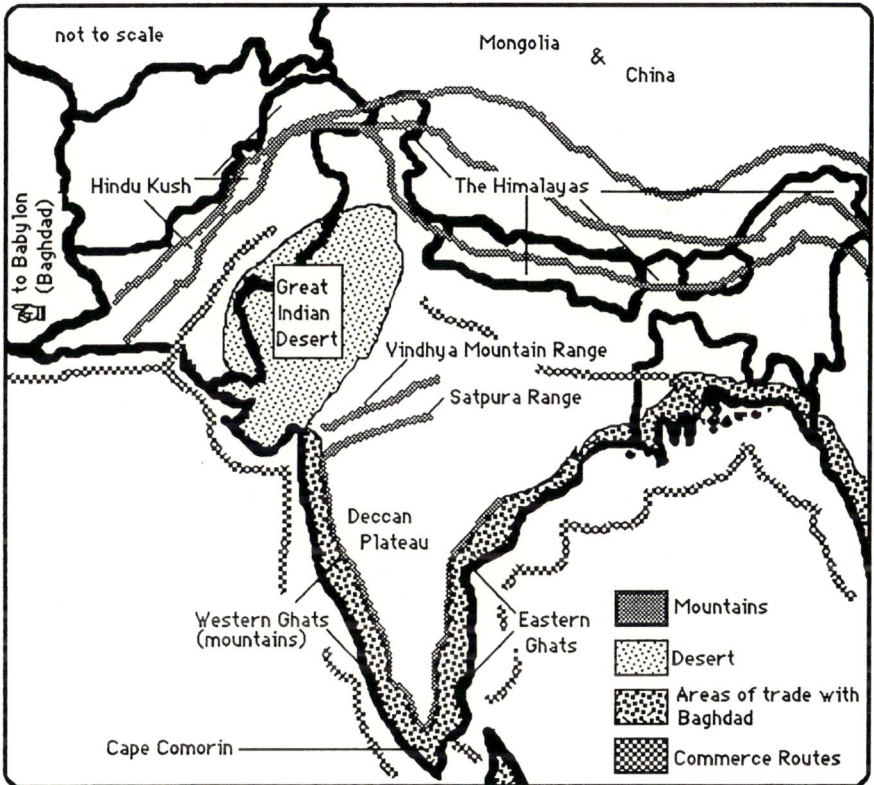

Figure 16
Physical Features and Water Commerce[139]

---

[138]K. M. Sen, pp. 15-18.

[139]"The World," Supplement to the *National Geographic*, December 1981, p. 780 A, Vol. 160, No. 6. *Bartholomew World Travel Map -- Indian Subcontinent.*

The Aryan Migration (circa 1500 BCE)

At some point between 2,000 BCE and 1,500 BCE the Aryan tribes entered India through Hindu Kush. The Aryans did not have a written language at this time. The Aryans are unquestionably the authors of the Vedic literature. (For centuries the writing down of the *Vedas* was expressly forbidden. The oldest known written version of the *Rig Veda* dates only to the fifteenth century of the Common Era.) The various texts were composed and handed down in an oral tradition. The Aryans were greatly skilled in warfare and brought with them the horse-drawn chariot. This was a terrifying method of making war and the indigenous tribes rapidly gave way to the invaders. The Aryans employed a large number of insulting terms for those whom they vanquished. They considered the customs of these peoples to be uncouth and immediately sought to convert them to the "proper" Aryan ways. The native peoples of Persia and India fell to this onslaught while a different group of Aryans pushed their way into Europe. The Aryans followed the path of the great rivers; the Indus and the Ganges (*Gange*) became the highways of their civilization (see Figure 17 - The Aryan Migration). They were skilled in agriculture and thus their expansion onto the fertile valleys and plains watered by the rivers was almost inevitable. The Aryans brought with them herds of oxen, sheep and goats and knowledge of cultivation. Small kingdoms developed and competed with one another. The great *Mahabarata* which includes some of the earliest songs of the Hindu literature is probably a development of stories about a local struggle between clans found along the Rivers *Ganges* and *Jumna*.[140]

The primary deities of the Aryan pantheon were not territorial and totemic, but rather elemental: the great god of water, *Indra*; the god of fire, *Agni*; the god of sky, *Dyauspitar*; the sun god, *Surya*; and dawn goddess *Usha*. There are even a few songs in the *Rig Veda* addressed to *Varuna*, prime mover of the universe and foreshadow of the post-Vedic *Brahman*.[141]

---

[140]Watson, pp. 21-37.

[141]Watson, pp. 30-39.

Alexander's Raid

One of the few dates which can be established with certainty in the history
of India is that of Alexander the Great's raid in 326 BCE Alexander entered India
through Persia with a great army. Arriving in the Indus valley through the Kyber
pass, Alexander summoned the kings and chiefs of the area to a council near
present day Kabul (in what is today Afghanistan). Many of these rulers accepted
Alexander to avoid the impending conflict with his army. However, one ruler
known to the Greeks as "Porus" gathered his forces at Taxila on the banks of the
Indus and sought help from other rulers to oppose Alexander. The two great
armies faced one another on the flooded plains surrounding the river Jhelum (see
Figure 18 - Alexander's Raid and Greek Control of India). After a great battle in
which Alexander's forces were victorious, Porus and Alexander became friends
and allies. The Greeks controlled all of the lands up to the Indus river, with Porus,
a strong ally, to the East. Alexander gathered his forces, marched South to the
Arabian Ocean, met his fleet there and returned to Persia by ship. He died in
Babylon the next year, with his dream of an empire stretching to the Indian ocean
unfulfilled. The contact and trade with the Greek Empire did have cultural and
musical implications for the Northern Indians. The *murchana* or modes of
Northern Indian music are identical with the modes of the Greek musical theorists.
Some writers argue that the Greeks influenced the Indians while others that the
Indians influenced the Greek. Neither view can be established with authority, but
certainly there was interaction.[142]

The Mauryan Empire

The Hindu kingdoms of North India were involved in many territorial
disputes before Alexander's Raid and in its aftermath. Though Alexander was
unable to unite India in his Empire, the Mauryan Empire succeeded in this by the
third century BCE The emperor Chadragupta and his son and heir Bindusura were
able to subdue most of India from the East to the West and as far South as the
Mysore Plateau.

---

[142]Watson, 18, 45-47.

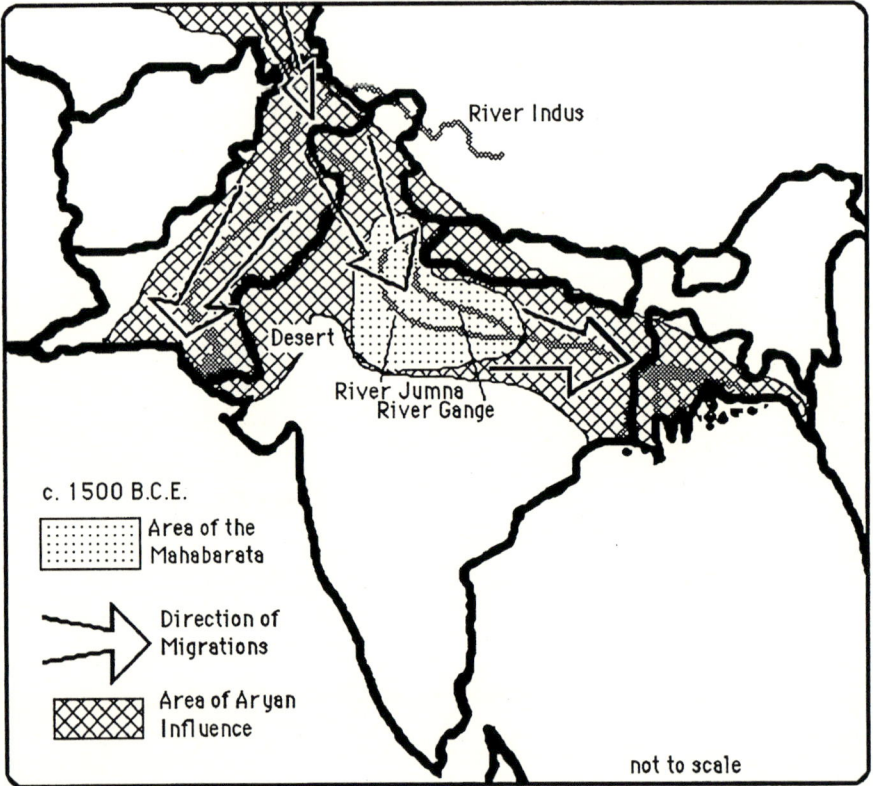

Figure 17
The Aryan Migration[143]

[143]Watson, pp. 30-32., Walter Imber and Hans Boesch, ed., *India* (New Delhi: Oxford and IBH Publishing Co., 1975), pp. 186-192.

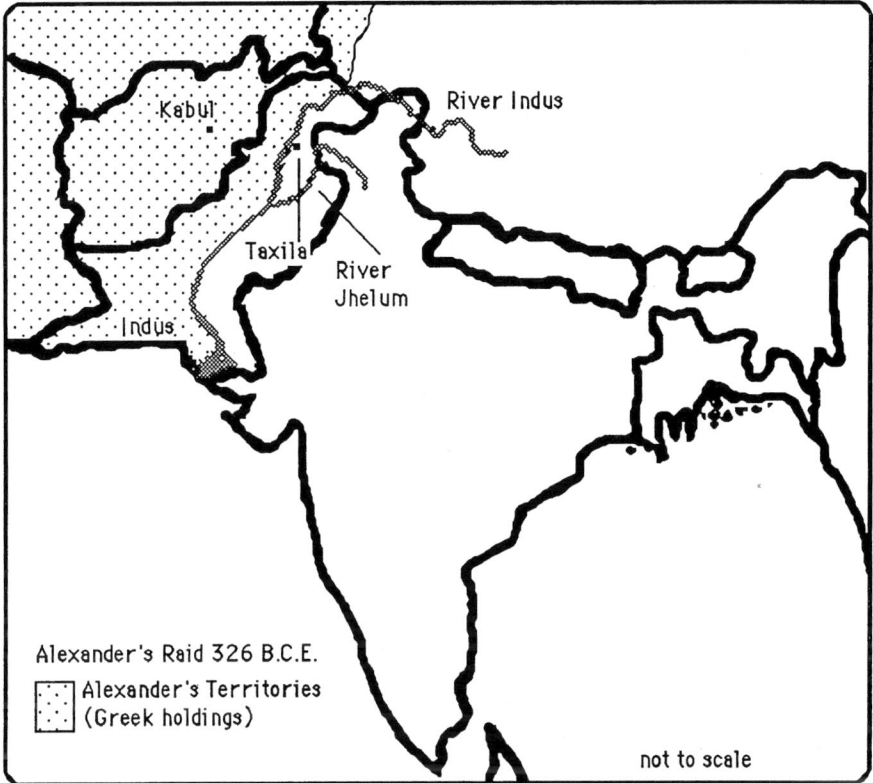

Figure 18
Alexander's Raid and Greek Control of India[144]

Bindusura left the Empire to one of his staff, Ashoka[145] (c. 273-232 BCE). The Nastika Hinduism reforms (which include the *Jain* and *Buddhist* religions) spread widely during the Mauryan Empire. Ashoka was himself a devout Buddhist, but he supported all the religious groups within his empire. The Mauryan Empire as ruled

---

[144]Watson, pp. 45-47.

[145]Ashoka had served as governor in both Taxila in the North and Ujjain in the South on the Deccan Plateau. Watson pp. 50-1.

by Ashoka included most of modern India[146] along with Pakistan and Bangladesh (see Figure 19 - The Mauryan Empire Under the Emperor Ashoka). The Empire established roads and a system of communication throughout Northern India. The dissemination of knowledge and art during this period did much to establish the foundations of Hindusthani music and art.[147]

Southern India, The non-Aryans

Though the various descendants of the Aryans had occupied most of India by the time of the Mauryan Empire, in the South the native Dravidians continued to rule their own lands. Ashoka pushed as far South as the central plateau, but not into the heart of the Dravidian South. At some point in time near 40 CE the maritime traders discovered how to use the great monsoon winds to travel directly from the Red Sea to the Southwest coast of India. When the winds reversed with the change of season, the ships could sail back quickly. This eliminated as much as two months from the travel time to or from Alexandria in Egypt to Calicut and other ports on the South Indian coast. (See above: Figure 16) This trade enabled the Southern Indians to maintain civilizations independent of the Aryan North. Water-based trade was established with the ports of the West and with areas of Indo-China.[148]

The Christian Faith Arrives in India

Tradition maintains that the Apostle Thomas traveled to India during the first century and established the Christian church on the seacoasts of the South. Thomas is also credited with establishing Christianity in the near eastern regions of Syria

---

[146]Ashoka took as the symbol of his authority a pillar topped by four lions which face the cardinal points, the Sarnath Lion Capital.

[147]Watson, pp. 47-51.

[148]Watson, pp. 71-3.

and Persia, throughout present day Iraq and Iran. The important trading links between these areas has already been discussed (see above Figure 16).[149]

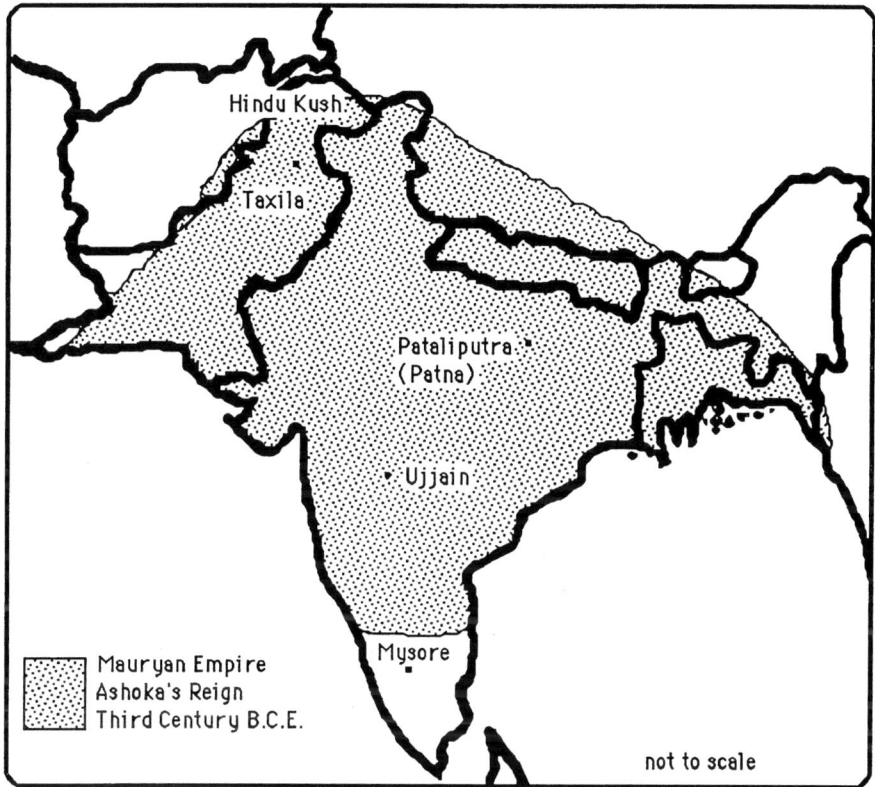

Figure 19
The Mauryan Empire Under the Emperor Ashoka[150]

---

[149]Most Rev. Stephen Neill, *The Story of the Christian Church in India and Pakistan* (Grand Rapids, Michigan: William B. Eerdmans Publishing Company, 1970), p. 16; Father Placid Podipara, C.M.I., *The Canonical Sources of the Syro-Malabar Church*, (Rome: Oriental institute of Religious Studies, 1986), p. 33; Most Rev. Ibrahim N. Ibrahim.

[150]Watson, pp. 47-51.

The Thomas Christians

Little is known of the first few centuries of the Christian church in India. The Indian Christians on the Southern coasts have been called by many titles: Syro-Malabar, Indo-Chaldean, Malabarian, St. Thomas Christians, Nazrani Mapilas, and Chaldeo-Malabarian. Syro-Malabar tradition maintains that the Church was founded there by St. Thomas the apostle; local Hindu tradition corroborates this assertion. The apostle is believed to have met a martyr's death at the hands of Hindus on the Coromadel coast (the West Coast of Southern India). A tomb believed to be the burial place of St. Thomas is held in veneration near Mylapore on the outskirts of Madras (see Figure 20 - Christian India).[151] Placid J. Podipara, C.M.I lists a number of the important events in the Church of the early fathers dating back to the earliest history of the Church even the Council of Nicea (John, Metropolitan of Persia and Greater India).[152]

It is interesting to note that, although St. Thomas himself is said to have established the Church in Southern India, the bishops of this Church seem to all be connected with the Persian See of Seleucia. Five copper plates record the privileges accorded to the Christian community and some others by a local ruler sometime near 800. The plates are in the old Tamil language, but include several unusual signatures by the witnesses. These signatures are in Pahlavi (a type of Persian), Arabic (in Kufi script), and Persian (in Hebrew script). This ruler gave slaves to the Christian community in Quilon. He also gave them the responsibility for customs, weights and measures and even the official seal of the kingdom. Though this community appears to have been foreign in origin, it became rooted in the soil of India. It appears that all the bishops for this community were nominated from Babylon until the Synod of Diamper.[153] [154] The language of the liturgy was that of Syria and these Christians retain their Syrian links to this day.[155]

---

[151]Podipara, pp. 49-50.

[152]Podipara, pp. 50-1.

[153]In 1923 Pope Pius XI consecrated the first Indian Bishop. In 1926 he published *Rerum Ecclesiæ* an important missionary encyclical emphasizing the need for indigenous clergy. *New*

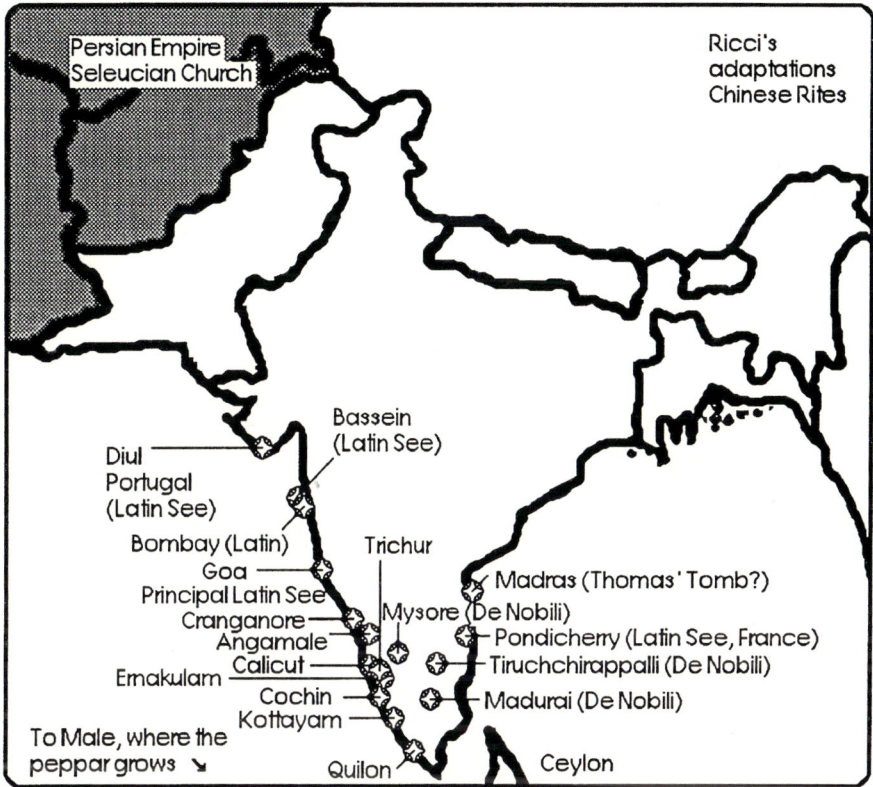

Figure 20
Christian India[156]

Catholic Encyclopedia, Vol. 7, p. 441.

[154]The only native Indian to be consecrated as a bishop before the twentieth century was Matthew De Castro, a Hindu convert, was consecrated as a Latin Rite bishop in 1637 by Francesco Ingoli who was the Secretary of the *Propaganda* in Rome. The original intention was to send Bishop Matthew to Ethiopia to work. This proved impossible and Matthew returned to India. Since his appointment had not been approved by the King of Portugal under the Padroado, the Archbishop of Goa would not recognize Bishop Matthew as a validly appointed or consecrated bishop. Matthew was recalled to Rome in 1658 where he died in 1677.

[155]Neill, pp. 16-19.

[156]*Harper Atlas of World History* (New York: Harper and Row, 1987), pp. 56-7, 117, 168-9, 177, 303; R. Montgomery Martin, ed, *The Illustrated Atlas and Modern History of the World* (London:

The Seleucian Church (Chaldeans)

Since the early Christian Church in India received its bishops from the ecclesial structure of Babylon, it is appropriate to examine the foundation of the Church in Babylon, the Church of Seleucia-Ctesiphon. This Christian community takes its name from the cities of Seleucia and Ctesiphon on either bank of a canal joining the Euphrates and Tigris Rivers near Baghdad. (See Figure 21 - The Syrian Connection.) It is also known in its various divisions as: the Church of the East, the Church of Persia, the Babylonian Church, the Assyrian Church, The East Assyrian Church, Nestorian (for their support of Nestorius), and Chaldean. Tradition holds that the Seleucian Church was founded by Mar Mari, who was a disciple of Mar Addai. St. Thomas (Mar Thoma) is reported to have sent Addai to Edessa. The Seleucians maintain that their Church was visited by both the apostle Peter and the apostle Thomas. Some maintain that St. Bartholomew is also connected with the Church in Babylon. The Seleucians report that their principal prelate was consecrated by the patriarch[157] of Antioch until persecutions and travel restrictions between the region made this impossible. At this point the Church in the West (Antioch, Edessa and Nisibis) granted them the authority to consecrate their own bishops and metropolitan.[158] At the same time the Jacobite (Monophysite) Church was divided into two distinct parts. The Syrian Patriarch of Antioch chose the ranking Metropolitan of Persia to become his appointed delegate in all matters. He granted the metropolitan the right to both appoint and consecrate bishops and metropolitans and to bless the holy chrism. This person became

---

John Tallis and Company, 1851) reprinted and edited as: *Antique Maps of the 19th Century World* (Hong Kong: Portland House, 1989), pp. 78-83; Catholic University of America, *New Catholic Encyclopedia* V. 7, (New York: McGraw-Hill Book Company, 1967), pp.435-441.

[157]In the East, a *patriarch* (who is also a *metropolitan*) has the right to appoint and consecrate bishops. In the West a *metropolitan* is a bishop who exercises authority over other bishops but who does not have the right to appoint and consecrate another bishop. All appointments come from Rome. *New Catholic Encyclopedia* , Vol. 9, p. 744.

[158]"Metropolitan" is a term often used in the Oriental Rites to refer to a bishop who exercises ecclesial authority over other bishops in his province. Archbishop, a Latin Rite term, may be applied to Archbishop-Major, *Catholicos*, *Maphrian* and Metropolitan since each of these exercises authority over other bishops. The term *Catholicos* applies particularly in the East because the *Catholicos* is allowed to make use of universal (*catholikos*) jurisdiction of the *Patriarch* he serves. *New Catholic Encyclopedia*, Vol. 9, pp 742-5.

known as the *Maphrian*, who served as the principal prelate. The *Maphrian*, the highest cleric in the East outside of Antioch, was given the privilege of consecrating and enthroning (not appointing) the Patriarch of Antioch.[159] The connection with

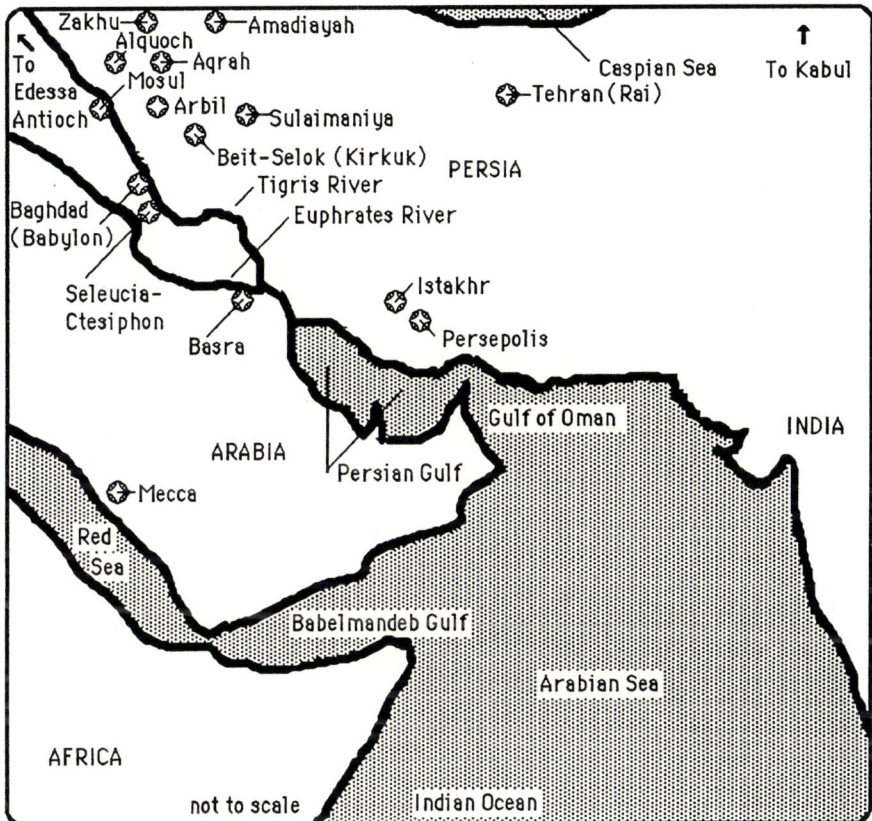

Figure 21
The Syrian Connection[160]

---

[159]The title of *Maphrian* is conferred today only upon the *Catholicos* (or *Maphrian*) of the Jacobite (Monophysite) Church in South India. Mafriana can be translated as "fructifier." It is derived "from *phrâ*, to make fruitful, beget." Adrian Fortescue,Ph.D., D.D., *The Lesser Eastern Churches* (New York: A.M.S. Press, 1972) reprint (London: Catholic Truth Society, 1913), p. 340.

[160]*Bartholowmew World Travel Map -- Middle East;* Newsweek, *Hammond Atlas of the Middle*

114

the Seleucian Church was continued through the arrival of the Latin Church with the Portuguese.[161]

The first historically verifiable bishop of Seleucia-Ctesiphon was Mar Papa bar 'Aggai who exercised his ministry at the end of the third and beginning of the fourth century.[162] In 345 Papa called a synod of local bishops in Seleucia-Ctesiphon (which was at that time the administrative center of the Greater Persian Empire). Papa attempted to organize the various churches throughout Persia with himself as metropolitan. The other bishops opposed him in this. Several claimed to have older Sees (Apostolic See) and maintained that they had their establishment from St. Thomas himself. In 410 Maruthas of Martyropolis in Armenia[163] called another synod with the permission of King Yazdgard I.[164] Maruthas served as the personal envoy of the Patriarch of Antioch. This synod accepted the Nicene Creed and established Seleucia-Ctesiphon as the Primary See in Persia, making it responsible for the metropolitans of Nisibis, Arbela, Beit-Selok, Beit-Laphat, Holwan, Kaskar, and some 30 bishoprics (See Figure 21 - The Syrian Connection). Another synod held in 420 subscribed to the canons as established in the West at the councils of Nicea, Ancyra, Gangra and Laodicea.[165]

East (Maplewood, New Jersey: Hammond Incorporated, 1991), pp. 14, 21, 24; Herbert G. May, ed., *Oxford Bible Atlas* (New York: Oxford University Press), pp. 52-3, 55, 67, 71, 75, 78, 79, 92-3. Rev. Alberto Colunga, O.P. and Rev. Laurentio Turrado,*Biblia Sacra iuxta Vulgatam Clementinam, Nova Editio* (Matriti: Biblioteca De Autores Cristianos, 1965), *Mapas -- Asia Anterior, Palestina, Asiriay, Babilonia*, p. 1258. Martin (*Antique Maps*) pp. 78-83.

[161]Podipara, pp. 33-4.

[162]Donald Attwater, *Churches in Communion With Rome* (Vol I of) The Christian Churches of the East, Revised edition (Milwaukee, Wisconsin: The Bruce Publishing Company, 1961), p. 188.

[163]Podipara names him Marutha of Maipharkat an Apostolic See suffragan to Edessa. This may have been the case at an earlier time. The appointment to the Armenian Church while serving as envoy for the Patriarch of Antioch seems more important, though either way an attachment to the Western Church is clearly evident. Podipara, p. 34.

[164]*New Catholic Encyclopedia*, Vol 13. p. 54.

[165]Podipara, pp.33-4.

In 424 a synod called in the city of Markabta by Mar Dadiso declared the Seleucia-Ctesiphon Church to be independent of the Church of Antioch. Many scholars believe that this was to calm the fears of the Persian Emperors, who were often in conflict with the Byzantine Empire. Any interference by the Byzantine Churches of Antioch, Edessa and Nisibis into Persian affairs was looked upon with suspicion and treated as treason. It was shortly after this that the prelate of the Seleucian Church began to use the titles *Catholicos*, *Catholicos-Patriarch* and *Patriarch*.[166] [167]

During the reign of Catholicos Baboe (456-484), Nestorian doctrines were introduced into the church. This was the work of Bar Sauma of Nisibis. In 486 a council under Acacius exhibited Nestorian tendencies while still proclaiming "perfect and indissoluble unity of the humanity and the divinity of Christ." This council also legitimized the marriage of priests. Another council in 497 extended the legitimacy of married clergy to include bishops and patriarchs. By the sixth century Nestorian theology was established as the norm. Some claim that this was a purely political response of the Church in the Persian Empire since the Empire was then at odds with Byzantium.[168]

During the seventh-century war with the Byzantine Empire, tradition says that the true cross of Christ was in Ctesiphon (614), where it had been placed after it had been captured in Jerusalem. The Mongol and Arab invasions were later to destroy the Church in Ctesiphon as well as most of the Nestorian Church. In response to the destruction of the city, the *Catholicos* Henanisho II (who reigned from 777-780) moved the Apostolic See to Baghdad. The Chaldean Church is a descendant of this See and is in explicit union with the Holy See in Rome.[169] The

---

[166]Podipara, p. 35.

[167]The "Second Letter of the Western Fathers'" is provided as evidence by the Seleucians for this break. It states that any judgement of the Seleucian Prelate is reserved to Jesus Christ. Podipara, p. 35. Most probably this is an apocryphal document. See also E. Khayyath, *Syri Orientales Seu Chaldæi Nestoriani et Romanorum Pontificum Primatus*, Rome, 1870, p. 5.

[168]Podipara, p. 36.

[169]Today the Chaldean Patriarch of Babylon in Baghdad has as suffragans the following places in

Nestorian (Jacobite or Monophysite) Church of the East continues to exist. The Jacobite Patriarch of Antioch supported the Syrian Christians of India during their struggles with the Society of Jesus (Jesuits).[170]

The Tamil South

The Shaivite Chola (rulers of Tanjore) and the Vaishnuvite Pandyas (rulers of Madurai), both devoutly Hindu, are two of the most enduring dynasties in the Tamil-speaking South. At various times each made war upon the other and upon neighboring kingdoms. The Cholas under Rajaraja I (985-1014) struck as far North as the great river Ganges. Marco Polo visited the Pandyas kingdom in 1288 and again in 1293 while working for the court of Kublai Khan. He commented most favorably upon the prosperity of the Kingdom of Madurai. In 1311 a force sent by a northern sultan sacked the beautiful city of Madurai and returned North to Delhi. The Dravidians realized the significance of this new threat. They resisted the coming invasion of the Islamic emperors from the North. On the banks of the river Tungabhadra in the middle of the Deccan, Vijayanagar ("city of Victory") was built in 1336. The great Hindu kingdom which took that name -- Vijayanagar -- became an ally of the Dravidians in their resistance. Until the middle of the sixteenth century this alliance held against the incursions of the Islamic rulers. (See figure 22 - The Tamil South and Vijayanagar.) The Syrian Christian Community existed during this time period, but did not attempt to wrest control from these

---

Iraq: Alquoch, Amadiayah (East of Zakhu, also on the Turkish border), Aqrah (East of Zakhu), Sulaimaniya (Northeast of Kirkuk) and Zakhu (on the Northernmost border with Turkey) as well as the Eparch of St. Thomas the Apostle in the United States of America. There is also a metropolitan in Kirkuk and archbishops in Arbil, Basra and Mossul. (See Figure 8.) *Annuario Pontificio*. Libreria Editrice Vaticana, Città Del Vaticana, 1989. p. 1043

[170]The current *Catholicos-patriarch* of the Church of the East (Nestorian Church) Mar Denha, IV resides in Chicago in the United States of America. Another Nestorian Patriarch resides in Baghdad, his community separated from the rest of the Nestorians when Patriarch Mar Shimun XXIII adopted the Gregorian (Latin) calendar. This second group maintains the name of the Church of the East or Nestorian Church. The current Chaldean Patriarch (Uniate, with the See still in Baghdad) is Mar Raphael I, Didawid. From a letter written to the author by the Most Reverend Ibrahim N. Ibrahim, Bishop of St. Thomas the Apostle, Chaldean Diocese, United States of America.

dynasties. Rather they supported and followed the laws as they existed. Karnatic Music developed and flourished in the Dravidian South.[171]

European Establishments

The Portuguese traders and missionaries had arrived in India before the coming of the Moghuls. Vasco da Gama established his trading footholds for the King of Portugal in 1498. The Portuguese mission of da Gama was invested with ecclesiastical and temporal rights by an exclusive Papal Bull.[172] This authorized Da Gama to search for converts to the faith as well as to trade for spices. Landfall in Calicut (a city on the Malabar coast) was achieved in 1498. Although there were followers of Islam and Syrian Christians established on the Malabar coast, the subcontinent remained primarily Hindu. From their base at Calicut (see Figure 23 - Principal European Trading Centers), the Portuguese established other trading missions on the subcontinent. The trade city of Goa was taken by force of arms in 1510. It became a great foundation for the Portuguese and "Portuguese" is still spoken there in the twentieth century, though not in an altogether familiar form. With the Portuguese came Latin Christianity. The existence of a Syrian Christian community both surprised and dismayed the Portuguese.[173]

The Syrian Christians welcomed their new-found Portuguese cousins with open arms. They acknowledged them as brothers in Christ and shared Eucharist with them.[174] The Portuguese missionaries established an ecclesial authority under the patronage of the King of Portugal. Under this system (the *Padroado*), the King of Portugal was authorized to establish all bishoprics in India. The Syrian

---

[171]Watson, pp. 83-85.

[172]This placed all of India under the *Padroado* (patronage) of the King of Portugal. See Podipara, p 57.

[173]Neill, p. 57. Watson, p. 105f.

[174]"*Communicatio in sacris*" Podipara, p. 57.

118

Christians posed a problem in that they already had their own dioceses and bishops (some six of them were recognized by the Portuguese and even granted financial subsidies).[175] The Portuguese attempted to Latinize the Syrians and to include them under the ecclesial authority of Portugal instead of the Seleucian Patriarch in Baghdad.[176]

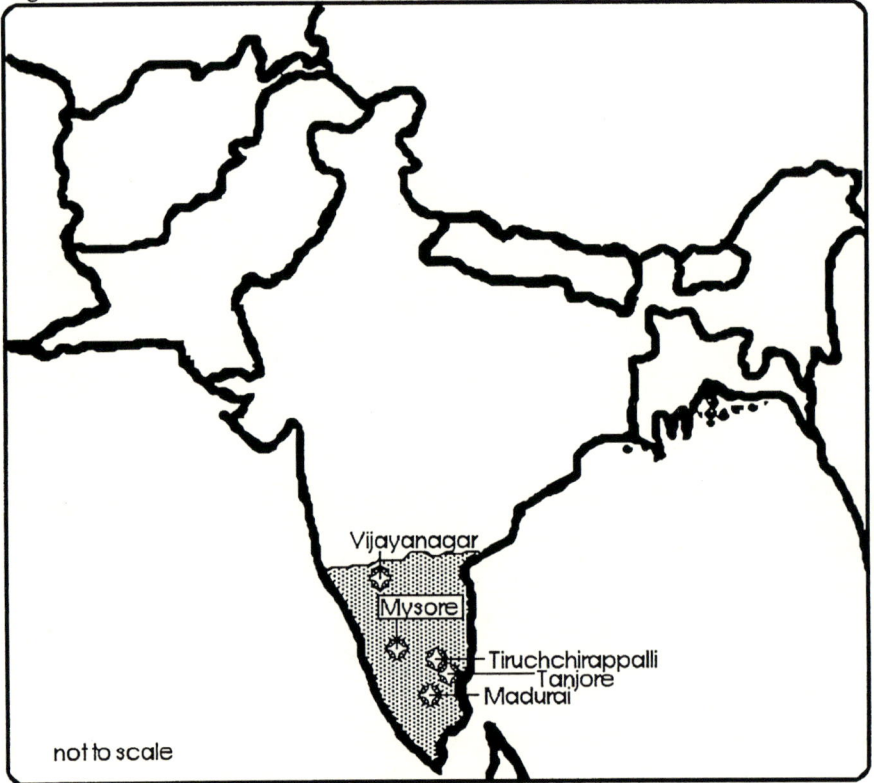

Figure 22
The Tamil South and Vijayanagar[177]

---

[175]Podipara, p. 57.

[176]Sadly, the Portuguese seemed not concerned with converting people to Christianity, but rather in making them into Portuguese Christians.

[177]Harper Atlas of World History, pp. 116-7, 168-9. Bartholowmew World Travel Map -- Indian Subcontinent.

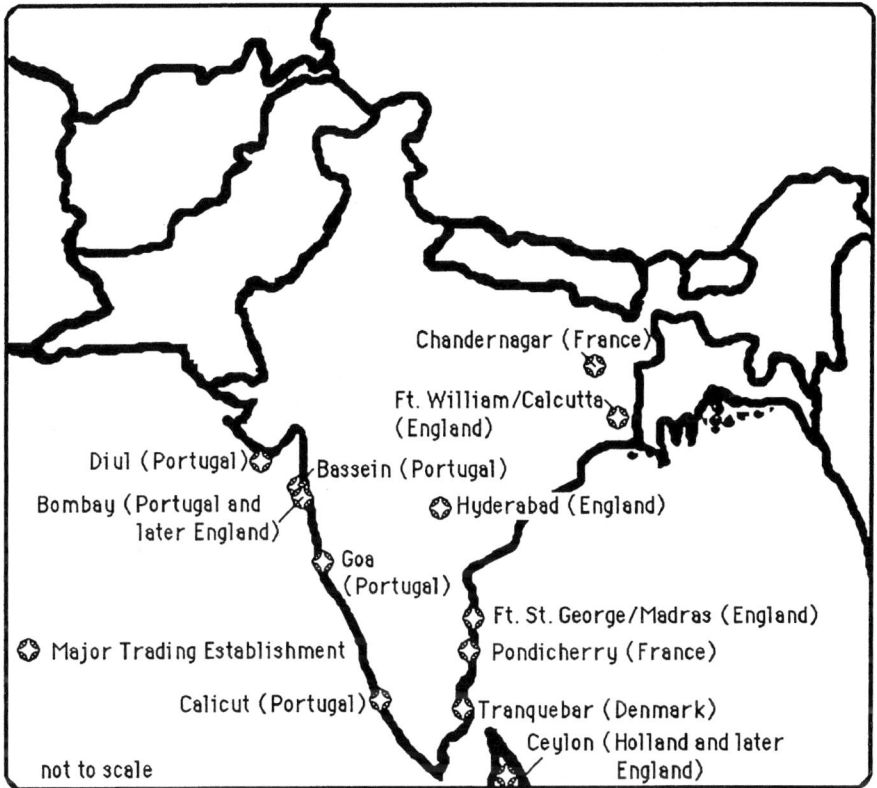

Figure 23
Principal European Trading Centers.[178]

The Portuguese catalogued and forbade the use of the adaptations the Syrians had made from Hinduism even though many of these were merely cultural and not religious. The Syrian community was accused of the heresies of Nestorius. They

---

[178]Watson, pp. 105-128, *New Catholic Encyclopedia* V. 7, pp.435-441.

were familiar with Nestorius, but examination showed that they did not exhibit his heresies.[179]

The struggle between Portugal and Seleucia became heated in the last half of the sixteenth century. Patriarch Abdiso (who had succeeded Mar Sulaqua) in 1556 sent two bishops to the Malabar Church. These were Mar Elias and Mar Joseph. They were accompanied by two Maltese Dominicans, Bishop Ambrose, O.P. and Rev. Antoninus, O.P. Father Antoninus was then serving as the Papal Nuncio in the East. They had been sent to Mar Sulaqa by the Pope. The Portuguese detained these men and would not release them for almost eighteen months. The two Seleucian bishops were forced to learn the Latin Rite and were released only when they agreed to work under the jurisdiction of the Archbishop of Goa (see Figure 20). Portugal claimed the See of Goa as the principal See in India; they considered the bishop of Goa to be "the bishop of Malabar and of the Whole of India."[180]

Patriarch Abdiso' sent his representative, Mar Abraham, to Rome. In Rome Mar Abraham professed his faith before the Pope and was then granted Papal credentials to teach the faith he had professed. In 1567 Mar Abraham arrived in Goa. (The Papal brief had assigned the See of Angamale to Mar Abraham with its historical connection to the Patriarch of Seleucia under Patriarch Abdiso'. The See of Gamila was entrusted to Mar Joseph.) Mar Abraham was made the principal prelate of the Eastern Bishops and Archbishops in India. The Portuguese accused Abraham of heresy and imprisoned him in Goa. He escaped and arrived in his See with the help of some Jesuits and the Latin (Portuguese) bishop of Cochin. Mar Joseph was also accused of heresy and deported to Rome where he died in 1569. This left Mar Abraham as the undisputed principal prelate of the East in India.[181]

Mar Abraham asked the Jesuits to work under his authority in Angamale. In 1583 he held a Synod there. He entrusted a seminary at Cenota to the Jesuits.

---

[179]Neill, pp. 33-5. Podipara, pp. 40-3, 56-7.

[180]Neill, pp. 34-7. Podipara p. 50.

[181]Podipara, pp. 57-9.

At the explicit request of Rome, Mar Abraham attended a council of the Latins in Goa in 1585. This council decreed many things including the translation into Syriac of the current Latin Rite as well as the correction of errors in the current Syrian liturgical books. The members of the council approved the catholicity of the Patriarch of Seleucia and his authority regarding Mar Abraham.[182]

At this time the Most Reverend Aliexo de Menezes received appointment as the Archbishop of Goa from the King of Portugal. He was strongly imbued with the Counter-Reformation spirit and insisted that all Christians should come under the explicit authority of the Pope. He saw this as fulfilled in India by including all Christians under his authority as principal prelate of India. In the last decade of the sixteenth century he began to maneuver things so that the Malabar Christians should fall under the Padroado.[183] Mar Abraham did not put into effect the decrees of the Goan Council of 1585. Because of this proceedings against Mar Abraham were begun in 1595, officially at the request of the Holy Father.[184] Before the official proceedings were begun in Rome, Mar Abraham had become reconciled with the Jesuits and petitioned through their superior general that his Archdeacon George be appointed coadjutor bishop with right of succession. The Jesuits requested that Archbishop Menezes postpone the official proceedings against Mar Abraham. In 1597 Mar Abraham died without having Papal approval of his successor. Archbishop Menezes sent the Jesuit Father Francis Roz, S.J.[185] to Angamale as Vicar Apostolic (*See vacante*).[186] Archdeacon George immediately took up the administration of the See. Soon thereafter, Menezes recalled Roz and allowed the

---

[182]Podipara, p. 59

[183]Podipara, p. 59

[184]A Papal Brief dated Jan 21, 1597, authorized Archbishop Menezes to appoint a Vicar Apostolic for the See of Angamale in the event that Mar Abraham had not nominated a successor. Podipara, p. 61.

[185]Roz was a Spanish priest and member of the Society of Jesus (S.J.). Podipara, p. 64.

[186]In a previous brief dated January 27, 1595, Pope Clement III had told the Archbishop of Goa to institute proceedings against Mar Abraham and to hold him in custody. He was also instructed to place a Latin Rite priest in the position of Vicar Apostolic and not to allow any bishop into India except as authorized by Rome. Podipara, p. 61.

archdeacon to administer the diocese. He sent the archdeacon advisors and required of him a profession of faith by a formula Menezes had devised. The archdeacon did not accept this immediately. The Portuguese civil and religious leaders in Cochin held a meeting at Vaipicotta and publicly stated that the archdeacon was a good catholic. The archdeacon assented to a verbal profession of faith there, but not the one Menezes had sent. Menezes was displeased and traveled himself to the Malabar coast. He preached vehemently against schism at Vaipicotta and commanded the archdeacon and the presbyterate not to include the name of the Patriarch of Seleucia in the Mass or in the Divine Office. This was done under threat of excommunication.[187] The archdeacon and the presbyterate yielded this point. Menezes continued to travel through the See where he exercised jurisdiction by celebrating the sacraments of Confirmation and Holy Orders.[188] The priests ordained were forced to condemn all heresy and promise obedience to Rome (through Goa).[189]

Finally having gathered a larger support group, Menezes forced Archdeacon George to surrender his authority in the See. The archdeacon was forced to agree to the following points paraphrased here:

1) Condemnation of Nestorius, Theodore and Diadore
2) Agree to follow the laws of Peter as interpreted by the Bishop of Rome
3) Profess faith as prescribed by Menezes
4) Destroy all previous books (all to be corrected or burned)
5) Acknowledge the supremacy of the Bishop of Rome (Pope)
6) Condemn the Patriarch of the Church of the East as a heretic and schismatic and swear not to have any relations with him[190]
7) To accept only bishops from Rome as approved in Goa by the Padroado
8) Obey Menezes until the arrival of the new bishop appointed by Rome

---

[187]*latæ sententiæ.* Podipara, p. 61.

[188]Both of these sacraments are reserved to the Apostolic See (local ordinary).

[189]Neill, pp. 34-7. Podipara, pp. 62-3.

[190]This Patriarch was Mar Denha Simon who was expressly in communion with Rome. Podipara, p. 63.

9) To convoke a synod in a place appointed by Menezes, accepting
everything that would be settled there, and to send to it
priests and representative laymen
10) To remain unescorted by guards, traveling only in the company
of Menezes and in the same vehicle.
Refusing to accept any of these conditions would be considered a
refusal of all.[191]

The synod was convoked in Diamper in June of 1599. Menezes convoked the Malabarians under pain of excommunication and some 130 clerics and 660 lay people participated. Menezes forced the Church in Malabar to accede to his authority. They promised obedience to Rome and to its bishop, and condemned the Seleucian Patriarch, Nestorius, Theodore and Diadore. The liturgy was entirely Latinized as were the theological books of the Syrian Christians. The Synod of Diamper ended the Syrian connection and the jurisdiction of the Patriarch of Seleucia in Malabar. On November 5, 1599 Father Roz, S.J. was appointed successor to Mar Abraham. Angamale was then made a diocese which was suffragan to Goa (December 20, 1599). On August 4, 1600, the *Padroado* of the Portuguese king was applied to Angamale.[192]

Syro-Malabar / Syro-Malankara

The synod effectively placed all the Malabarians under the Padroado of Portugal. The Latin Rite was completely in control of India. In 1637 Archdeacon George died and Thomas, his nephew, took over leadership among the Syrian Christians. In 1652 a bishop from Seleucia arrived in Mylapore with letters from the Pope. This was Mar Ahattalla, "Patriarch of All India and China." The Portuguese did not allow him to stay, but sent him on North to Goa via Cochin. The archdeacon Thomas and many followers went to Cochin demanding to examine

---

[191]"Cf. Roulin F. *Historia Ecclesiæ Malabaricæ cum synods Diamperitana.* Romæ, 1745 Pp. 511 of. Podipara p. 62.

[192]Neill, pp. 35-6. Podipara, pp. 71-4.

the credentials of Ahattalla. Many of the Syrian-Christians were told that the bishop had drowned on this journey.[193]

Believing that the Jesuits (and the Portuguese authorities) had murdered their new bishop, a great many of the Syrian presbyterate and the Archdeacon Thomas gathered at Mattamcherry. On Friday January 3, 1653, they tied a rope to the famous Coonan Cross and each one took hold of it, symbolically touching the cross. They then swore an oath never to serve under the Jesuits. On May 22, 1653 the discontented met at Edapally. Twelve priests imposed hands upon the archdeacon and pronounced him Archbishop Mar Thomas I.[194] Many did not approve of this saying that Rome had not agreed to such an action. Those who remained united with Rome through this separation constitute the Syro-Malabar Rite of the Catholic Church. Those who followed the Archdeacon developed into the Syro-Malankara Rite which was not reunited with Rome until the twentieth century.[195]

The Coming of the Protestants

Shortly after the Portuguese, other European powers came to India, primarily Protestant countries which ignored all Papal Bulls. The Dutch, French and English each had a lasting effect on India, as did the Turks and Afghanis from the North. The British with their East India Trading Company were to have a lasting effect greater than they had anticipated. In the mid-seventeenth century the British began their trading establishments in India. For almost 150 years they were to remain as merchants, not as rulers.[196] (See Figure 23 - Principal European Trading Centers).

---

[193]Neill, p. 36.

[194]In the absence of a Patriarch this was considered by them to be canonically legal, the authorization having come, they reasoned, from Mar Ahattalla.

[195]Neill pp 36-7 Podipara, pp. 77-0, 82-3.

[196]Neill, pp. 48f. Watson, pp. 118f.

Islamic and European Expansion

The Turkish and Afghani followers of the prophet Mohamed swept into India from Persia around 1525. The great Moghul empire (See Figure 24: The Moghul Empire) under Akbar united most of the North into a single domain, though it did not reach nearly as far South as had the empire of Ashoka.[197]

The English and the French colonial powers struggled for the domination of India after the fall of the Moghul empire. The struggle culminated in the *Raj* of Great Britain, when the sun never set upon the British Empire. It may be important to note that the British Raj did not interfere with religious matters, which were seen largely as the responsibility of the local rulers. Islamic, Hindu and Sikh kingdoms continued to exist. Where Christianity had been accepted in any form, it was interfered with only slightly by the British authorities (the various Catholic Rites ignored the British entirely). Though the Church of England was encouraged and supported, it was not granted a monopoly.[198]

The reign of Queen Victoria can be seen as the culmination of the British Empire in India. In 1876 she was proclaimed the Empress of India. It was in 1911 that King George V traveled to India where he was hailed as king-emperor by the great princes of the realm. He announced that the capitol of the Indian Empire would be moved from Calcutta (headquarters of the East India Company) to Delhi, historic center of leadership. It must be noted that education in English, Persian, Arabic, Sanskrit, and other indigenous languages was encouraged by the British. Telecommunications with telegraph and rapid mail services were also established as were the now famous railways of India. It was also British rule and education which brought about the foundation of the Congress party whose first meeting was in Bombay in December of 1885.[199]

---

[197]Watson, pp. 105-127.

[198]Watson, pp. 118-127.

[199]Watson, pp. 129-147.

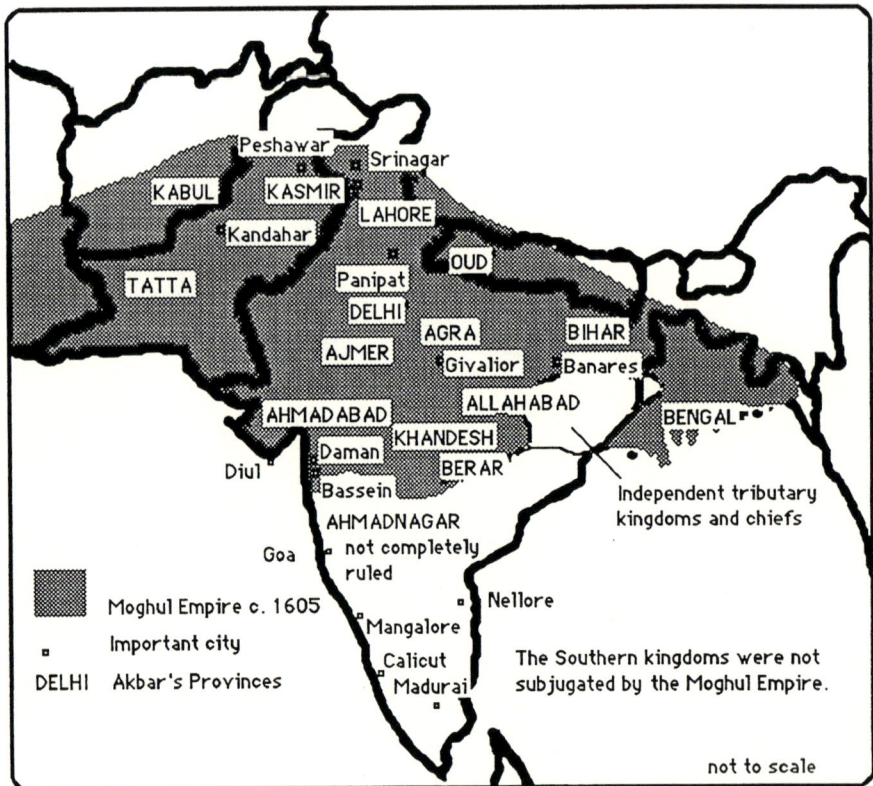

Figure 24
The Moghul Empire[200]

Syro-Malankara History to Reunification

The Syro-Malankara[201] group under Mar Thomas I[202] broke entirely from
the Portuguese and retained the ancient Eastern Rite as it had been practiced until

---

[200]Adapted from Watson p. 112.

[201]*Malankara* is another term for Southern India. *New Catholic Encyclopedia*, Vol. 9, p. 103.

that time. 32 Syrian congregations broke and followed Mar Thomas, while 84 eventually returned to communion with Rome. Mar Thomas appealed to the Jacobite (Monophysite) Patriarch of Antioch. The patriarch sent a bishop to Kerela in 1665. The new bishop refused to consecrate Thomas. Five successive Mar Thomases were to exercise authority over the Malankarans until 1772 when two bishops sent by the Jacobite patriarch were to consecrate Thomas VI as Mar Dionysius I. The Malankarans eventually adopted many of the practices of the Antiochean Church even though they had staunchly refused to adopt Latin ones under the Portuguese. Various attempts at reunion with Rome were made, beginning with Mar Dionysius I. Circumstances did not allow full reunion until the twentieth century. Mar Ivanos, among others, petitioned Rome for reunion. On September 20, 1930 Mar Ivanos and Mar Theophilus made professions of faith and were received into full communion with the See of Rome. The Congregation for Oriental Churches made it very clear that the Syro-Antiochean (Syro-Malankara) Rite was to be preserved and that it would not be merged and or confused with the Syro-Chaldean (Syro-Malabar) Rite.[203] By the second Vatican Council great strides had been made in the reunion. Many Syro-Malankara bishops were in attendance at the council. The Malankarans had maintained a basically West-Syrian Rite, but they had substituted Malayalam for Syrian as a liturgical language. Rome had approved of this upon reunion and established that Malayalam was an official liturgical language. The Syro-Malabar, upon learning that Malayalam was an official liturgical language petitioned the Congregation for Oriental Churches for permission to use it in their liturgics. This permission was granted and both the Syro-Malankara and the Syro-Malabar Rites were using the vernacular before the Second Vatican Council. Bishops of both Rites spoke eloquently at the Council in favor of the use of vernacular languages in the liturgies of the Church.[204]

---

[202]Thomas Palakomatta, Attwater, p. 169.

[203]Attwater, pp.169-171.

[204]Father John Edapilly, C.M.I. interview by the author, Tape 6.

The Syro-Malabar Rite

Under the excessive Latinizations of the Portuguese, the Syro-Malabar Rite was almost lost. In 1887 two Vicarates Apostolic (Tricur and Kottayam) were erected to allow ecclesial separation for the Orientals from the Latins though they were administered by Latin prelates. In 1896 three Vicarates Apostolic, Trichur, Ernakulam, and Changana-cherry, were established under Malabarian prelates. By 1917 the Malabarians were placed under the Congregation for the Oriental Church (Rome) and in 1923 the hierarchy was restored with Ernakulam as the Metropolitan See. To the present there are three hierarchies in India, one for each of the following: the Latin Rite (Roman), the Syro-Malabar Rite (East Syrian), and the Syro-Malankara Rite (West Syrian). Some confusion is caused in the overlapping of these dioceses and their jurisdictions.[205]

Syro-Malabar Liturgy

With the erection of the Syro-Malabar Hierarchy in 1923, the Malabarians began to restore their ancient Chaldean Rite along with the adaptations which had been made to it during the centuries. For example: There is no wedding ring. Rather the groom ties a small golden cross (*tali* or *minnu*) to the neck of his bride. The thread which holds this cross is drawn from the bridal veil. This is similar to the Hindu *thali*, though the cross with 21 beads is distinct from the Hindu. Much of the paraphernalia of the Malabarian Church is similar to that of the Hindus. The use of gestures and vestments from both Syria and India continue to this date.[206]

---

[205]*New Catholic Encyclopedia.* Vol. 9, pp. 92-7.

[206]Attwater, pp. 200-203, S. G. Pothan, *The Syrian Christians of Kerela* (Bombay, India: Asia Publishing House, 1963), pp. 69-71.

The Malabar Rites Controversy

One notable effort towards inculturation was that of the Jesuit priest Robert de Nobili, S.J. Working in Madurai (see Figure 22) in the early seventeenth century, he introduced an adaptive method of evangelization which had been introduced into China by Rev. Matteo Ricci, S.J. In this method, the Christian missionary did not expect his converts and neophytes to become Europeans. Instead, the missionary became incul-turated. As far as could be allowed, native customs were retained. Father De Nobili took upon himself the saffron colored robes of a *sannyasi* (a Hindu Ascetic). He ate as the Indians did and studied the Vedic (and *Bhakti*) literature. This allowed him to converse with the Brahmin caste whom he had undertaken to evangelize. Father de Nobili allowed his followers and converts to use traditional Indian customs which he decided were of a civil rather than religious nature. This included such things as the *kudumi* badge (a symbol of the *Brahmin* caste), the sacred thread (another *Brahmin* caste symbol), the *santal* (mark on the forehead), and the usual and ritual ablutions of the *Brahmin* caste (such cleansings are vital in the hot climate of Southern India). The *Brahmins* of Madurai accepted Father de Nobili's method and many were converted. The Portuguese distrusted de Nobili and accused him of desecrating the faith by introducing non-Christian rituals and sacramentals. He argued using the words of St. Paul and St. Thomas Aquinas. After many investigations the dispute was submitted to Rome and to Portugal. In 1621 Martins de Mascarenhas, Grand Inquisitor of Portugal, decided in Father De Nobili's favor. In 1623 Pope Gregory XV in his constitution *Romanæ Sedis* also decided in favor of the adaptations. The Jesuits renewed their efforts by establishing two groups for evangelization: the *sannyasis* to work amongst the upper castes and the *pandara swamis* to work amongst the lower castes and those who had no caste. The missions in Madurai, Mysore and Tiruchiapaly were very successful using these methods.[207]

In 1703 Charles Thomas Maillard de Tournon, *legatus a latere* of Pope Clement XI, arrived in India on his way to examine the Chinese Rites. Tournon decided against sixteen points of adaptation which had been in use until that time.

---

[207]Neill, pp. 38-41.

With the controversies renewed, arguments for both sides carried on for years. Pope Innocent XIII appointed a special Congregation to decide the matter. The Congregation was headed by Prospero Lambertini.[208] On December 12, 1727 the decision of Tournon's decree was confirmed by the Holy See. In 1734 Pope Clement XII in his brief *Compertum exploratumque* again confirmed this sixteen point condemnation. The papal bull *Omnium solicitudinum* of Benedict XIV published on December 12, 1744 brought the matter to a close. All priests were bound by an oath in sixteen parts, which forbade the previous practices.[209]

True to their vow of obedience to the Pope, the Jesuits took the oaths required of them. They did obtain permission to designate missionaries to the service of the caste-less ones. This particular dispensation ceased to exist in 1773 with the suppression of the Jesuits. Pope Pius XII reviewed the controversies over the Malabar Rites and the Chinese Rites. On December 8, 1939 the Chinese oath was done away with. On April 9, 1940, those missionaries serving in India were no longer required to take the Malabar Rites oath. As mentioned earlier, the Second Vatican Council was to renew the stand of Father De Nobili on inculturation.[210] [211]

---

[208]Lambertini was later enthroned as Pope Benedict XIV. *New Catholic Encyclopedia*, Vol. 9, p. 98.

[209]*New Catholic Encyclopedia*, Vol. 9, p. 98.

[210]*New Catholic Encyclopedia*, Vol. 9, p. 98.

[211]The Jesuit Major Seminary in Pune (attached to the Papal Seminary J.D.V.) is named for Father De Nobili.

INDEX

ROMAN CATHOLIC STUDIES